MONEY FOR THE ASKING: FUNDRAISING IN MUSIC LIBRARIES

**Music Library Association
Basic Manual Series**
Jean Morrow, Editor

1. *Music Classification Systems* by Mark McKnight (2002)
2. *Binding and Care of Printed Music* by Alice Carli (2003)
3. *Music Library Instruction* by Gregg S. Geary, Laura Snyder, and Kathleen A. Abromeit (2004)
4. *Library Acquisition of Music* by R. Michael Fling (2004)
5. *Audio and Video Equipment Basics for Libraries* by Jim Farrington (2006)
6. *A Manual for the Performance Library* by Russ Girsberger (2006)
7. *Money for the Asking: Fundraising in Music Libraries* by Peter Munstedt (2012)

ML
111
M73
2012

MONEY FOR THE ASKING
FUNDRAISING IN MUSIC LIBRARIES

by

Peter Munstedt

Co-published by

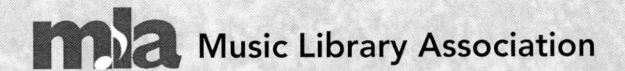

mla Music Library Association

and

A-R Editions, Inc.
Middleton, Wisconsin

Library of Congress Cataloging-in-Publication Data

Munstedt, Peter Alan.
   Money for the asking : fundraising in music libraries / by Peter Munstedt.
     p. cm. — (Music Library Association basic manual series ; no. 7)
   Includes bibliographical references.
   ISBN 978-0-89579-734-6
 1. Music libraries. 2. Library fund raising. 3. Music librarianship. I. Title.
   ML111.D73 2012
   025.1'1—dc23
                                                     2012002591

ISBN 978-0-89579-734-6

A-R Editions, Inc., Middleton, Wisconsin 53562
© 2012 All rights reserved.
Printed in the United States of America
1 3 5 7 9 10 8 6 4 2

TABLE OF CONTENTS

Acknowledgments	vii
Introduction	ix

Chapter One: Getting Started with Fundraising — 1
Initial Steps	1
Working with a Development Office and Music Department	3
Promoting the Library	7

Chapter Two: Four Steps in Working with Individual Donors — 11
Identification	11
Cultivation	15
Solicitation	22
Stewardship	27

Chapter Three: Types of Donations — 33
Gifts in Kind	33
Monetary Gifts	36
Planned Giving	36
One-Time Donations for Special Projects	39
Endowments	39

Chapter Four: Fundraising Events in a Music Library and Elsewhere — 43
Library Benefit Concerts	43
Book Sales	47
Other Public Events	51
Private Events for Major Donors	52

Chapter Five: Corporations, Foundations, and Government Grants   55

Overview   55
Institutional Approval   55
Corporations   56
Foundations   57
Government Grants   62
Other Grant Opportunities   66

Chapter Six: Issues to Consider in Fundraising   69

Hidden Costs   69
Institutional Politics   71
Ethical Concerns   73
Conclusion   77

Appendix 1: Case Studies from the MIT Lewis Music Library   79

Library Renovation   79
Library Newsletter   80
Class of 1982 Music Library Fund   81
MITSO Recordings   83
Oral History Project   84
Collection Endowment   85
Violin Music Donation   86

Appendix 2: Donation Information on Selected Music Library Websites   89

Notes   103

Bibliography   115

Books and Articles   115
Web Pages   121

Index   125

ACKNOWLEDGMENTS

As a music librarian, I am extremely fortunate to have worked with librarians and development staff who encouraged my interest in fundraising. Only with their assistance and coaching was I able to conduct fundraising activities as part of my music library work. Early in my career as a music librarian at the University of Missouri–Kansas City, the director of the UMKC Libraries, Ted P. Sheldon, encouraged me to pursue fundraising, especially grant writing. At the Massachusetts Institute of Technology, my fundraising interests were further supported and deepened. Thanks to Ann Wolpert, director of the MIT Libraries, for her support of my fundraising activities. My supervisor for eighteen years, MIT humanities librarian Theresa Tobin, consistently advocated for my fundraising endeavors and allowed time for me to research this book. The current and former development personnel for the MIT Libraries, including Anne Marie Michel, M. J. Miller, Sharon Stanczak, Jos Wanschers, Steven Horsch, and Toni Green, along with MIT's director of arts development, Glenn Billingsley, were mentors who provided me with a wealth of information and served as role models of professionalism.

Writing this book was possible only with the generous support of several individuals who read parts or all of this manuscript. They strengthened the book with their own special expertise that compensated for my shortcomings. The Lewis Music Library's collections support associate Christina Moore provided adept editorial assistance along with insights from a music library perspective. Two development staff members from the MIT Libraries provided invaluable help. Jos Wanschers contributed many excellent suggestions and clarifications. Steven Horsch provided meticulous and especially generous assistance in describing several areas in the development field that were outside of my experience. Development staff members from the New England Conservatory, Marian Alper and Francesca Giannetti, read portions of the book and provided constructive advice. My gratitude also goes out to two editors from MLA's Basic Manual Series. Jean Morrow, director of libraries at the New England Conservatory of Music, was instrumental in producing this book. She provided extensive input, especially on grants, along with remarkable editorial facility and extraordinary generosity in guiding this book. Deborah Campana, conservatory librarian at Oberlin College, skillfully edited the final manuscript to make it more decipherable. I would like to acknowledge James L. Zychowicz, A-R Editions, for his facilitation throughout the publishing process, along with Richard Griscom for his thorough copyediting of the text.

Other people who assisted with this book include: Linda Solow Blotner, Gary R. Boye, Melanie Brothers, Ashlie Conway, Ana Dubnjakovic, Ellen Duranceau, Robert Follet, Charlene Follett, Tracy Gabridge, Steven Gass, David Gilbert, Alan Green, Ellen T. Harris, David Hursh, Lisa Hooper, Carolyn A. Johnson, Forrest Larson, Leonard Lehrman, Peter Linnitt, Kathryn Logan, John Lubrano, Nobue Matsuoka-Motley, Deb Morley, Jennifer Oates, Jennifer Ottervik, Ned Quist, Marian Ritter, Brian Robison, Michael Rogan, Roy Rudolph, Maurice Saylor, Brad Short, Judy Tsou, and Elizabeth Walker. I also appreciate the support of other members from the MIT Libraries staff and the Music Library Association.

Finally, I am most grateful to my family. Thanks to my children Kurt, Emily, and Karl for their patience and understanding during the writing of this book when I would sometimes disappear to do *my* homework. And special gratitude goes to my wife, Anne, for her steadfast support and encouragement. You cannot thank donors enough, and that principle goes double for caring wives!

INTRODUCTION

Although not likely to appear in most library school curricula, the subject of fundraising deserves serious study by any librarian who wishes to augment the library's material and financial resources and to increase, as well, the library's visibility in the surrounding community. Successful fundraising can supplement substantially the library's annual operating budget. At the same time, fundraising activities can be a significant tool in marketing the value of the library's services and collections to its patrons.

Much has been written to assist the general librarian with fundraising. Very little information is available, however, that is directly geared to the specific circumstances of those who work in music libraries or with music collections. *Money for the Asking: Fundraising in Music Libraries* promises to fill this serious gap in the professional literature. The seventh volume in the Music Library Association's Basic Manual Series, this book informs the music librarian about a variety of practical fundraising activities that can take place in even the smallest music library setting. As most librarians who work with music materials quickly discover, the love of music can attract a wide range of potential supporters to the music library's cause, giving the music library a distinct advantage over the general library. Fundraising activities can run the gamut, from the smallest solicitation to a private donor to the development of a major grant application for submission, to a wealthy philanthropic institution; all types of fundraising endeavors appropriate for the music library will be discussed fully in this book.

Conceived as a comprehensive guide for the music librarian inexperienced in the area of library fundraising, the manual begins with a general overview of the topic. A lengthy discussion of the interrelationship between good library service, promotion of the library, and fundraising follows. Several chapters deal with solicitation of individual donations and the steps involved in cultivating strong donor relationships. All types of donations are examined, including one time monetary gifts, planned giving, and endowments. Throughout the book, the author emphasizes the fundraising opportunities that are unique to music libraries and the kinds of fundraising music activities that have been successful in music libraries. His chapter on corporate, foundation, and government grants steers the music librarian in the direction of those institutions and agencies most likely to consider music library projects for funding.

Librarians rarely embark on fundraising efforts in a vacuum. Major portions of this book will educate the music librarian about institutional politics and on how best to approach senior administrators. Considerable discussion focuses on the potential impact on both the staff and library services when the music librarian participates in fundraising.

The author writes from his fundraising experience in a small music library located within a large university setting. Much of what he has accomplished over the years, however, can be achieved in the very smallest of institutions. Although a music library within a university has the benefit of access to a larger, professional fundraising staff, the music library in a smaller institution may be at a distinct advantage in having considerably less competition from other departments when seeking institutional support for its fundraising project.

There are many issues to consider before the music librarian begins to undertake fundraising for the first time. Above all, one has to weigh seriously the benefits of ongoing fundraising activities against the potential drain on the library staff's time and energy and the overall efficiency of library operations. But as the author's years of experience clearly prove, the rewards of successful fundraising for any size music library are almost always worth the effort.

Jean Morrow
Founding Editor, MLA Basic Manual Series

Chapter One

GETTING STARTED WITH FUNDRAISING

INITIAL STEPS

With shrinking budgets and dwindling resources, not many libraries have the luxury of ignoring fundraising. Academic libraries, in particular, have put increasing emphasis on fundraising in recent years to supplement their regular operating budgets and to support special projects. A survey of the Association of Research Libraries member libraries in 2006 indicated that 92 percent of those libraries responding had a formal library development program.[1] Music librarians may find that their annual budgets are insufficient and that obtaining external funding is the only way to accomplish their goals. In challenging economic times, supplemental income through donations helps to buffer a library from budgetary reductions. Yet the percentage of music librarians who actively conduct fundraising work appears to be relatively small. The *MLA Survey of Personnel Characteristics, 2009 Report and Statistical Summary* asked music librarians about the broader category of "Marketing/Sales/Fundraising" in their jobs. Of the 264 Music Library Association (MLA) members responding to this question, 30 members list this area as a primary responsibility, 56 members regard it as a secondary area, and 178 members have no responsibility in this kind of work.[2] Those music libraries with fundraising initiatives already in place are probably benefiting from their efforts. Other music libraries, however, may participate only peripherally in institutional fundraising or development activities.[3] The music library staff may hear about major donations bestowed upon other libraries within their university and at music libraries around the country. They wonder if their music library should attempt to enter this enticing world of fundraising, but where to begin?

Fundraising is not a course taught frequently in library school.[4] It is a subject that librarians—especially administrators—often learn on the job out of necessity. Fundraising is commonly considered to be an art because it requires not only a practical knowledge of the field but also a keen intuition about human nature along with the ability to respond properly in delicate situations. The current scholarly literature contains a wide array of books and articles on library fundraising, although few resources specifically target music libraries.[5] In addition, increasing numbers of resources on the internet discuss general library fundraising.[6] With demanding workloads, however, most music librarians lack the time to dig through these materials. Fundraising is one discipline that is easy to postpone. This book aims to assist those music librarians who find themselves in this position. The perspective of this book is that of a music librarian rather than a professional fundraiser. The academic music library is the primary audience but public library fundraising activities will also be described along the way. Chapters will cover some of the basic concepts of fundraising, offer practical advice, and point out situations specific to music libraries.[7]

Financial Landscape

The first step to getting started with fundraising is to survey the financial landscape of your library. Here are a few questions to consider:

- Does the music library receive the funding it needs for materials and operational expenses?
- Is the library's physical space in a condition that properly serves its users?
- Does the collection sufficiently support the music curriculum and the needs of the university community?
- Is there enough staffing to accomplish the work?
- Are there special projects that need funding?

Some might question why librarians would contemplate raising money, especially in support of essential services. After all, institutional and library administrators should provide the necessary funding for a library. It is their job to obtain this money.[8] By all means, investigate these channels first. Fundraising may not be necessary if you receive a sufficient budget to accomplish your library's needs. However, if you are like most music librarians, adequate funding is not always available to your library, and fundraising is an option at least to consider.

Initiation of Fundraising Activities

The next task in the preparation for fundraising is to determine if initiating fundraising activities is a possibility for the music library. Examine the organizational structure of the development office at your institution, keeping in mind that fundraising is a team effort that requires cooperation among many workers and departments. Do not be timid and give up before you ask, assuming that the answer will be negative. This could be a sensitive area and you might be told to shy away, especially if the music library is not a high priority in the university's fundraising mission. On the other hand, your supervisor may be open to your request, especially if you bring forward a specific project with a budget, tangible benefits, and possible donors. Such a proposal will generate more consideration than a vague notion about adding money to a library budget. With a realistic project, your participation in fundraising could be greeted with enthusiasm by the library's upper administration and the development office, both of which might welcome your assistance in their common quest to raise funds for the library. If you are told that librarians do not conduct fundraising work, ask if the development staff could raise the money for you, or perhaps, allow you to assist in the work. Of course, every music librarian's situation will be different, but a well-considered and assertive request could yield a positive response.

Political Awareness

As you move forward with your initial development efforts, be cautious about the politics involved with fundraising at your institution. Any time there are people fighting over money—with their jobs depending upon the outcome—the inner politics and competition can be intense. The development field has even been compared to a poorly functioning work family: "Whether management is centralized, decentralized, or a hybrid model, all of these structures have a human element, so by their very nature they are at least somewhat dysfunctional."[9] Be forewarned, and always make sure to go through the proper channels within the university's organizational structure. Keep in mind that fundraising in many academic institutions is set up as a remarkably hierarchical system. For example, an individual with a vast giving potential becomes the "property" of a development office prospect manager. Only that manager has the right to approach the donor. If you wish to contact this potential donor, you must receive clearance first from that person's prospect manager. Such stringent rules exist for a reason. The institution must present a united and coordinated front when approaching donors. When in doubt, send any fundraising questions to your supervisor or development representative. Do not walk naively into a situation that could be potentially damaging to you and your library. Anyone who wants to play the fundraising game must follow the proper channels of authority. The development world is sometimes unfamiliar to those of us in the library profession, so proceed with caution if you are allowed to continue at all.

Role of the Library Director

The ultimate direction in library fundraising for most music libraries will likely be provided by the library director (or dean), who establishes the library mission and sets fundraising goals.[10] The library director has a broad perspective of fundraising possibilities and participates in the larger fundraising efforts on campus that the institution is undertaking or planning. As Samuel T. Huang, associate dean for external relations at the University of Arizona Libraries, points out, "The library dean plays a crucial leadership role in library development and fundraising. It is the dean's responsibility to be an advocate for the library at the deans' level and to convince the president and provost, the central gifts office and key volunteers to redirect or expand their interest. Nothing is as detrimental to library development as having key university administrators who are indifferent to the library's role and students' needs."[11] The library director also approves specific fundraising activities within the library system. One hopes that the library mission statement will encourage librarians to play an active part in development work and that job descriptions reflect this time commitment. The library administration should recognize the vital contribution that librarians' subject expertise plays in fundraising and communicate any development initiatives that might have an impact upon library staff.[12]

WORKING WITH A DEVELOPMENT OFFICE AND MUSIC DEPARTMENT

Development Officers

Most likely, an academic institution will have a development staff member whose responsibilities include the music library. This person may be on the university library staff, a member of an institution's central development office, or a combination of both. Your connection with this individual will be crucial to the success of your fundraising efforts. You will want to form a robust symbiotic relationship. The librarian needs donors to fund new projects while the development person looks for endeavors to fund and the subject expertise to support them. In an ideal situation, development staff and music librarians form strong professional and personal bonds as they work toward a common goal. Often this is the case, but there also exist inherent differences between these two job positions. Music librarians are responsible for providing and making accessible music appropriate to their music department and the institution's community. Those librarians in public services work closely with faculty and students. Music librarians possess a master's degree in library science, and they usually have one or more degrees in music. Raising money is not ordinarily in their job descriptions and it is often the last thing on their minds. Library development officers, on the other hand, rarely have a library science degree.[13] They normally possess an undergraduate or graduate degree. Area of study varies widely among development professionals, ranging from science and engineering to the arts and humanities. Many people come from sales and marketing, customer service, or other outreach-focused backgrounds to perform frontline development work. Development personnel that work in the area of planned giving often have legal backgrounds. Some development staff obtain certification after five years of professional fundraising experience through CFRE (Certified Fund Raising Executive) but this credential is not a requirement in the field.[14] Newly hired library development staff may lack in-depth knowledge of libraries and will depend upon library staff to learn subtleties of the library profession. Because they work in administrative positions, development staff members tend to have much less contact with students and faculty than library staff.

Because of these differences, there can be misunderstandings and even resentment between the two professions. Some librarians feel that any degree of perceived salesmanship on their part is repugnant to their training as librarians. They may prefer to ignore fundraising altogether. Librarians may wonder why the university administration cannot find funding for the library so that they can be left alone to conduct their librarian responsibilities. They may also resent the higher salary that development officers often earn. Development staff members, on the other hand, can become frustrated with librarians who hesitate or refuse to help them. They ask how library fundraising can take place effectively without assistance from the library staff. Development staff may also feel misunderstood by some librarians who fail to appreciate the high level of skills required for professional development work.

In spite of these inherent disparities and potential conflicts, library development professionals actually share many of the traits found in librarians. Both employees are service-oriented individuals who want to improve peoples' lives through their work. Some of them land their jobs after studying initially for another career path. On-the-job training is how both professionals often fine-tune their crafts. Development officers and music librarians belong to professional organizations through which members stay in close touch with each other.[15] Development officers in academic libraries can join the Academic Library Advancement and Development Network (ALADN), while academic development professionals often join the Council for Advancement and Support of Education (CASE) or the Association of Fundraising Professionals (AFP).

For music librarians, the Music Library Association (MLA) is their primary organization. They may also participate in the International Association of Music Libraries, Archives and Documentation Centres (IAML) as well as other organizations, such as the American Library Association (ALA), Association for Recorded Sound Collections (ARSC), and other music-related and library associations. Music librarians should recognize the similarities they share with their development colleagues and view them as allies with whom they can combine forces. Victoria Steele, as the head of the Department of Special Collections at the University of Southern California Libraries, summarizes this connection:

> The key to a successful library fundraising program is a synergistic relationship between development professionals and librarians. Development staff cannot succeed without the creative input of librarians, and librarians cannot achieve their vision without the practical assistance of talented fundraisers. When either side of the partnership is weak, results are mediocre, and the program can actually *lose* money. Though some workplace relationships can survive imbalances, development is not one of them.[16]

Development officers are usually glad to find a librarian who understands the development field and who is willing to identify potential donors, write clear proposals, and work to bring money into the library. After all, the librarian will be helping the development staff do its job. When both parties trust each other and understand their roles, this partnership can form a potent combination and result in successful fundraising that will benefit the library. The music librarian should continually educate the development staff about the library, its needs, and how it serves its constituency. When development representatives talk to potential donors, they should be able to speak intelligently about the music library and be cognizant of the ways in which a donor's interests could match those of the library. Unfortunately, development workers tend to be fairly mobile and they move frequently from job to job. Staff turnover in the development office makes it challenging for the music librarian who must establish working relationships all over again with each newly hired person.

Music Department

Once your institution gives you the go-ahead to begin fundraising and you recognize the complexity of fundraising politics within your institution, you are ready for the next challenge: working with the music department and their development personnel. The political minefields can be even more precarious and explosive in this environment. What could be at stake here is the music librarian's relationship with the music department, an affiliation that is critical for the proper functioning of a music library. After all, the primary mission of an academic music library is to support the curriculum and needs of the university's music department. The music librarian must stay in close touch with the current and future directions of the department. Under the right conditions, music departments view the music library staff as "one of their own" in a camaraderie that reflects their common knowledge and love of music. There is no stronger ally on campus for a music library than its music department.

A challenge to keeping cordial ties to one's music department occurs when the music library attempts to raise funds in direct competition with the music department. To some extent, this situation is inevitable, because both parties will be seeking donors (usually alumni) with interests in music. The music librarian faces what appears to be an adversarial position with the music department. This should not mean, however, that the music library will suddenly lose all of the goodwill it had garnered over the years with the music department, nor should this relationship necessarily create a confrontational situation. The outcome will depend on the individuals involved and the organizational structure of the institution. In some cases, one development person will be responsible for both the music library and the music department. That person will decide how to divide up present and potential donors. If the development person is fair and responsible, both sides should receive their equitable share. The situation becomes more complicated when there is one development person representing the music library and another development person looking out for the music department. On the face of it, this appears to be an "us versus them" state of affairs. The two parties, however, should understand that they have common goals. Raising money for the music library certainly benefits the music department and vice versa. It is understandable that both sides will want to retain exclusive rights to most if not all of their major donors, but there could be smaller donors that each side might be willing to share, especially for one-time solicitations. Your hope is that these development staff will work cooperatively to the advantage of the music library. For some smaller libraries and academic departments, it especially makes sense to join their limited forces and collaborate on development work. Their common interests and goals form a strong and natural alliance.[17]

In my experience, the development officers of the MIT School of Humanities and Social Science and Provost Office along with the faculty of the music department have been responsible for some of our music library's most significant fundraising projects, even though the library employs different development officers. A total renovation of the music library occurred when the associate provost for the arts (who was also a music professor) obtained funding from a major donor. The development officer working with the associate provost also solicited additional donations to complete the work. Without this support, we would probably still be sitting in an outdated library facility. Of course, the music department is thrilled to make use of the new music library and enjoy the benefits of this fundraising. Another example involves a large number of reel-to-reel tapes donated to the music library from the conductor of the MIT Symphony Orchestra. The library wanted to preserve these recordings and make them accessible. Having no money in the budget for this work, only fundraising would make the project possible. The development officer working for the music department obtained the names of alumni who had performed in the orchestra and generously shared these names with the library. The alumni were contacted and soon funded the project. These two projects benefited both the library and the music department. (For more details about these projects, see appendix 1.) Fortunately, the music department and the library worked together for a common goal. This is not to say that these rosy scenarios are necessarily the norm. It is not unusual for academic departments within a university to compete fiercely with each other for every fundraising dollar.

While the relationships between the development staff in the library and music department vary from one institution to another, the music librarian's role remains the same. Librarians should promote their fundraising causes in convincing fashion to the appropriate development staff, pointing out the benefits that the music library provides both to the music department and the wider community. When the music library's fundraising goals overlap those of the music department, the librarian should be sensitive to any conflicts that might arise. By working cooperatively with a music department, the music library's relationship may not deteriorate but can even strengthen over time. Also keep in mind that the central development office has its priorities for the present year and into the future. Similarly, the library administration and music department will have their own fundraising goals. You will need to determine where the music library fits into the bigger development picture on campus.

PROMOTING THE LIBRARY

In an economic environment in which libraries increasingly have to battle for institutional support, music libraries need to promote their services in order to retain a competitive edge. Whether we are aware of it or not, promotion of the music library occurs each day in the library, regardless of fundraising efforts.

ROLE OF LIBRARY STAFF

The library staff promotes the library positively to its constituencies by providing excellent services and collections. More active approaches advance the library's services through such means as a newsletter, e-mail, blogs, Twitter, Facebook, and events. Tailor your promotion to suit the needs of various constituencies. For an academic library, the primary targets are students, faculty, staff, and alumni. It goes without saying that a library would cease to exist without the active involvement of students and faculty. The library must promote itself in ways that will entice them to take advantage of the library's services. Promotional information might highlight recent additions to the collection, the latest music databases, availability of music notational software, or even the acquisition of new furniture. This practical information publicizes the library to encourage its use. Library and university staff members, on the other hand, require different specifics. The university library administrators, such as the music librarian's supervisor and other high-level administrators, demand bottom-line data. Information for them might include such aspects as library usage statistics, assessments of library activities, testimonials from users, and assurance that the music library deserves the budget that it receives.

IMPORTANCE OF ALUMNI

Alumni who have pleasant memories of the music library are the main constituents who will support your fundraising efforts. Alumni do not want to know the nitty-gritty of a library's operation; library hours and detailed budgets do not interest them. They need to understand, however, that the library remains a vibrant place on campus that is worthy of their contributions. Promoting the library to loyal alumni with this consistent message is essential for successful fundraising. As public relations director of the Queens Borough (New York) Public Library, Sue Fontaine reminds us, "Just as a product with no name acceptance that meets no particular consumer need and has no active marketing plan is unlikely to sell, an organization with no recognition factor, no identifiable, loyal clientele and no effective public relations plan will have a difficult time raising funds."[18]

In addition to promoting a positive image, the library needs to inform alumni that it actively seeks monetary donations. Potential donors look for attractive giving opportunities, so the staff should not be timid or embarrassed to publicize its needs. Donors will not contribute to your library unless they know that you can use the money. If your library has a specific fundraising project in mind, make a convincing case for its funding. Show all proposals to the development office which may promote them for you. The right proposal could resonate immediately with the development staff that keeps track of donors' interests. If a project requires major funding, the development office could add it to a list of university library or campus-wide fundraising priorities that seek to locate matching donors. In other cases, a library may look for general donations without specific projects in mind. Publicizing the names of current donors (except, of course, those who have asked that you not) and explaining the benefits of gifts will show potential supporters that the library appreciates donations and spends them wisely.

INTERACTION OF SERVICE, PROMOTION, AND FUNDRAISING

From a broader management perspective, promotion plays a fundamental role in the total fundraising picture. A close interconnection exists between three library operations: service, promotion, and fundraising. These functions create a cycle in which each component leads to the next. Excellent service is essential for any library and the key to successful fundraising. Users appreciate helpful service and a well-run library. They remember the high-quality service that the library provided them as students, and the library should remind them that this level of service still exists today. With effective promotion, alumni are ready to respond to fundraising requests. As the library receives monetary donations, a greater budget allows the library to enlarge and improve its services. The library promotes these better services, which in turn raise more money. And so this three-part cycle continues and expands. It takes time to get the cycle rolling, but funding will increase incrementally as the library recruits more donors and as established supporters augment their contributions over the years (see fig. 1).

Promotion through public relations and marketing is a discipline that involves specialized expertise and sophisticated techniques. Detailed discussion of these areas is beyond the scope of the present study.[19] Yet these subjects interact closely with fundraising activities. In fact, fundraising is sometimes described not as a separate organizational function, but as a specialization of public relations.[20] If your library employs or works with a public relations specialist, try

Service
- Good service is essential for a library's existence
- Library's goal is to meet users' needs
- Users appreciate and remember good service

Fundraising
- Effective promotion leads to successful fundraising
- An active and engaged library appeals to donors
- Increased funding can result in improved services

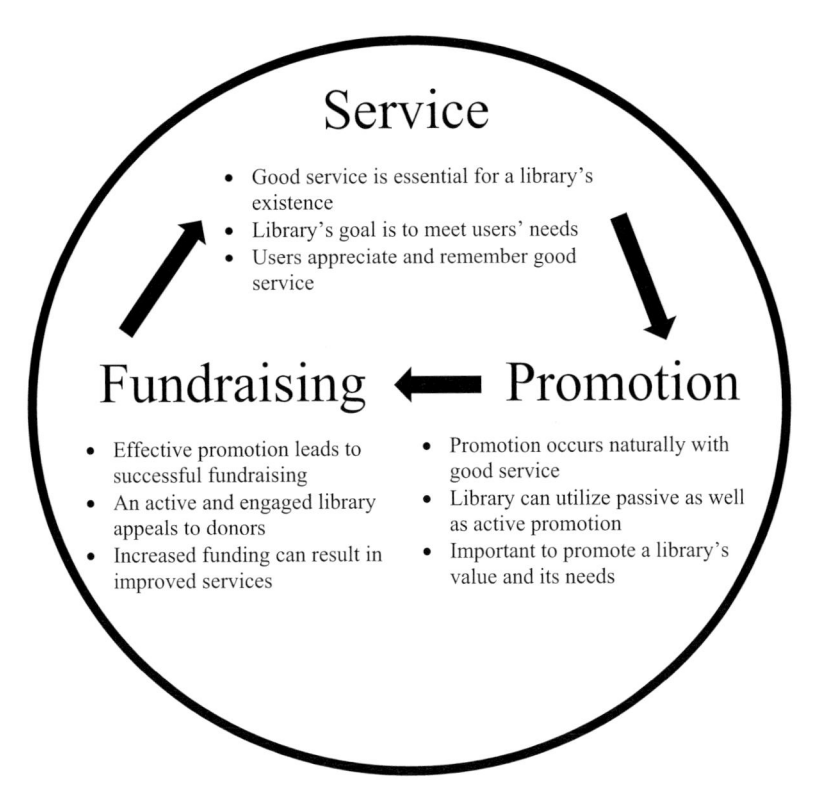

Promotion
- Promotion occurs naturally with good service
- Library can utilize passive as well as active promotion
- Important to promote a library's value and its needs

Figure 1. Fundraising cycle showing the roles of service and promotion.

to contact that person for professional assistance in your promotional work. These specialists often work closely with the development office in designing external communications. They may have limited time, but if they are willing to help, you could receive invaluable professional advice on promoting your library. For successful fundraising to occur, the library needs to publicize the library in as many ways as possible. With this in mind, the next chapter will examine some practical ways to attract potential donors.

Chapter Two

FOUR STEPS IN WORKING WITH INDIVIDUAL DONORS

In 2010, the amount of charitable giving in America, including both grant-giving organizations and individuals, totaled over $290 billion. Of that amount, approximately 73% of the donations came from individuals.[1] With the possibility for such funding, it is wise to consider individuals as potential donors for the music library. Fundraising professionals describe the process of raising money from individual donors in terms of four distinct steps: identification, cultivation, solicitation, and stewardship. You must complete each step before you take the next one. This chapter will concentrate on ways to obtain primarily monetary gifts from donors.

IDENTIFICATION

The first stage in the process of finding donors is to identify those individuals who have enough interest in your library to give you money. The development world refers to possible donors as "prospects." Academic libraries serve a well-defined constituency, including the institutions' students, faculty, staff, and some outside users. All of these individuals are potential prospects, but the primary base from which to draw is the university alumni. Some people may claim that university libraries have a distinct disadvantage in fundraising on campus because they do not "own" the alumni from any particular academic discipline. Academic departments keep track of their alumni and have a certain ownership of these constituencies. Libraries can argue for a claim over this entire constituency, however, since they serve all departments and therefore appeal to alumni from all academic disciplines. Some alumni have strong and positive connections to a particular department, and they prefer to donate in that direction. Not all alumni, however, have pleasant recollections of their academic rigors. The time spent away from studies may have generated their warmest and most enjoyable memories. These experiences may influence alumni to contribute to other causes on campus, including the libraries.

Consider the unique position of music libraries on a campus. Music libraries primarily support the teaching curriculum, research, and performance needs of the music department, but they also provide materials for recreational listening, reading, and performing. Unlike most subject-specific libraries, the music library appeals to the entire university community. After all, how many people do not enjoy some kind of music? Alumni from a wide range of disciplines outside of music may have warm feelings toward the music library and the times they spent there. Compare this to a mathematics library, for example, which attracts a fairly restricted clientele. Not many majors from nonmathematical disciplines visit there. It is not unusual, however, for mathematics students to frequent a music library to pick up a CD, watch a DVD, or check out a book or score. The music library serves as a source of relaxation, inspiration, and escape from other academic studies, helping to preserve the sanity of countless students. Users also obtain answers to research questions from library staff who are often passionate about music and who possess an in-depth knowledge to assist them. Students might also visit the music library virtually and enjoy the library's online resources, especially products such as streaming audio and video. Music library staff may not realize that their library holds a special place in the hearts of so many in the larger community, even those individuals who never enter the library doors. All of these factors give music libraries an edge over other academic libraries in competing for fundraising dollars.

Building a Mailing List

Many users will enjoy your music library over the years, but rarely do they tell you how much they appreciate the services you provide. Students use the library, graduate, and are never heard from again. The challenge is to locate and keep track of those alumni who would gladly earmark their donations for the music library if they only knew that it needed assistance. They may be out there, but how do you find these potential donors? One way is to start a mailing list in order to send news about the library to these individuals on a regular basis, in electronic or printed form—or both. This engages them once more with the music library. One effective starting point is to compile a list of alumni who currently use your library and ask their permission to join your mailing list. (You can always do this in your first mailing.) These individuals most likely appreciate the music library and may be willing to make a donation if asked appropriately. Add all music library donors to this mailing list as well. Also include on the list for your news mailing the music faculty along with faculty and staff from other disciplines, including emeriti professors, who have a strong bond to the music library. Note that many institutions discourage the solicitation of faculty and staff who have not self-identified as donors to the music library; be sure to confirm with your director of development whether or not solicitation of faculty and staff is allowed at your university before mailing direct solicitations to these people. Retired faculty members sometimes like to pay back a library for its many years of assisting them with their teaching and research needs. Current music faculty members are more likely to donate gifts in kind—such as CDs, DVDs, scores, and books—rather than money. You can cast an even wider net by asking your development officer if you may add to the mailing list the names of board members of music and arts organizations on campus. Members of advisory councils to the library and the music department are also potential donors who are worth contacting. If there is a library friends group, see about adding members' names to your list. When outside visitors show an interest in your library, obtain permission to add their names to the mailing list as well. If possible, put a signup sheet for the mailing list at the music library circulation desk and on your library's home page. You may gain some friends that you had not known previously. The internal mailing-list records should document such basic information as name, contact information, year of graduation (if appropriate), amounts and dates of donations (if applicable), musical interests, and connection to the library. Such a list helps the library staff keep track of all contributions and donors over time.[2] During this process, stay in close touch with the development office, which has detailed information about all donors to the university. Development staff may be willing to manage your mailing list in order to save you time. Always obtain clearance from the development office before you contact anyone on the mailing list, even if you are just promoting the library. If your relationship with the music department's development staff members is especially strong and you are feeling brave, ask them to share the names of music alumni for your mailing list. Do not expect them, however, to simply hand over their complete inventory of prospects. More likely, you will need to build your own list of donors slowly over time.

STUDENT ASSISTANTS

Current students will be your most frequent users, but they obviously should not be considered as prospects. It cannot be overemphasized that the music library staff should never view its users as just potential donors. You should not compromise service in any way because of fundraising efforts. (This topic is discussed further in Chapter Six under "Ethical Concerns.") With this in mind, consider contacting the music library student assistants once they graduate. Library student assistants can form a strong loyalty to the music library. They see the library's inner workings, get to know the staff, and realize the significance of the library on campus. Before they graduate, the music library may want to thank them in some way, such as a pizza party or even a small gift. Ask these graduating students if the library may add their names to the library's mailing list. Some will be happy to be included. By staying in touch, the library will probably receive donations from a few of these students. Contributions may be small at first but they often increase significantly as the personal wealth of alumni expands and their fondness for the library grows over time.

CAMPUS RESOURCES

There may be campus resources, such as student organizations, academic departments, or faculty members, that have potential for library donations. Do not expect lavish amounts of money, but keep in mind that small and consistent donations can make a difference in a music library's budget. Try to match the needs of the music library with the interests of these groups and individuals. For instance, the university Chinese Club may receive annual funding that it spends to promote Chinese culture on campus. Members of that club might be delighted to purchase books, scores, or recordings of Chinese music for the music library. Another possibility is to contact faculty members who are writing grants and ask if they will include a library component in their proposals. The Media Department at the University of Maryland, Baltimore County, made such connections on campus and increased its collections budget nearly 1,000 percent from 2003 to 2008 by actively approaching the Friends of the Library, the Student

Government Association, campus academic departments, and faculty members.[3] Contacting wealthy donors and applying for major grants may be the way to obtain substantial funding, but more modest donations are often just waiting for you in your own campus backyard.

MAJOR DONORS

Identifying and gathering names by these means is an effective way to develop donors and generate funding over a period of years. From a donor's perspective, smaller gifts have the advantage of being quick and easy tax deductions not requiring a major commitment.[4] You may even develop a major donor from these modest beginnings. This kind of funding, however, would not be sufficient to support a large-scale project requiring millions of dollars. Cultivating hundreds of small donors with limited giving capacity is not the answer in that case. In fact, the fundraising literature often states that 90 percent of the money a library raises is given by 10 percent of its total donors. Some research shows that this figure may be closer to a 95-percent/5-percent ratio.[5] Receiving a substantial donation from one or very few donors falls under the category of major giving.

Major donors are those individuals with many thousands and even millions of dollars to donate. These are the donors that fundraisers aspire to approach for funding, and because of their wealth and potential to give, such donors are popular targets for fundraisers. Obtaining institutional clearance to contact these individuals can be difficult and often impossible. If a music library project requires major funding, the librarian should ask the library's development representative about adding the proposal to the fundraising priorities of the library or university. If accepted, the development office will try to match this proposal with a potential donor. After presenting as much information as the development staff request, the librarian will need to wait and hope for a donor, since it will be the development office's responsibility to find the donor. As other development projects receive funding, your request should move higher up on the priority list. Gentle reminders from the librarian that are within reason and not to the point of irritation should continue until funding arrives. The process of locating a donor can take months or years, which may test the patience of the music librarian.

Keep in mind too that donors will sometimes surprise everyone and contribute towards a project regardless of where it stands in an institutional priority list. When this occurs, the institution is unlikely to turn away the donation even if the project is not high in its priorities. Money does have a way of talking. Of course, because the price tag of a major-gift proposal is so high, there is always the possibility that the library will never find a donor and the proposal will not obtain funding. By positioning the music library's needs onto the institution's list of fundraising priorities, however, you may succeed in landing a major one-time donation that will forever change your music library. Such an achievement takes persuasiveness, perseverance, and a little bit of luck.

Librarians may dream of finding a major donor on their own. Most of us have heard the tale of a disheveled old man in tattered clothes who shuffles into the library (usually public) every day and sits at the same table quietly reading magazines. The library staff treats him respectfully over the years but knows nothing about his background. Upon his death, as the story goes, this man turns out to have been an eccentric millionaire who leaves several million dollars to the library. Unfortunately, such elderly library-loving misers can be difficult to locate.

Central development offices keep active databases of likely prospects by researching and rating individuals according to their financial capacity and potential to give. They track donors' giving histories along with their philanthropic interests. A capacity rating system often assigns a number (for example 1–5) to each donor so that the donor's estimated giving potential is readily apparent. Development officers also compile "contact reports" which summarize any meetings or discussions that they have had with donors. This information provides a historic context about the donor that can be shared with other development staff. A database of these reports also supplies useful information through "data mining," which searches certain terms in order to ascertain donors' interests. With such sophisticated methods of analyzing donors, the music librarian is unlikely to discover a millionaire alumnus who escapes the radar of the central development office. Even if such an individual were to be located, the development office could have other projects in mind and may not give you clearance to contact that person at all.

ECONOMIC ENVIRONMENT

Over the years, the nation's economy and a library's budget will fluctuate. A financial downturn should not discourage music librarians from building a base of potential donors. Fundraising is a long-term process. Loyal donors who are in the habit of contributing regularly should continue to provide support. Some studies even suggest that donations to nonprofits actually increase during difficult economies.[6] In such times, it helps to remind donors of their critical importance to a library that faces harsh budgetary constraints. Let them know that donations play an essential role in supplementing funding for the library.[7] Inform them that their donation is an investment that provides real benefits and payoffs, and that most if not all of their donation goes directly to the library. In uncertain financial climates, such a claim will reassure donors that at least one of their investments will be a safe bet.

CULTIVATION

There is a saying in the development field that people do not give to things or ideas, they give to people. The heart of fundraising from individual donors involves the personal relationships that form between donors and library staff members. Cultivation involves these personal connections that develop over time. A warm and open relationship between donor and library staff is essential in cultivating fundraising dollars. The library informs and educates prospects about the library and shows them the ways in which their donations will benefit others. Cultivation is critical for effective fundraising, and it can be one of the most rewarding personal experiences of this work. Lifelong friendships can even develop when donors and librarians establish a dynamic bond based upon mutual respect and their common commitment to the music library.

It helps to imagine this relationship from the donors' perspective. They want their money invested wisely for a worthwhile cause. Donors must have total faith in the library staff to entrust a donation in its hands. Alumni donors also want to reconnect with their alma mater and to pay back an institution that changed their lives. Their donations allow them to actively participate again. Both the donor and library win in this situation.

Competing for Donors

Music libraries will be competing for donations not only against other departments at their institution, but also against many outside philanthropic causes.[8] The number of nonprofit organizations in this country nearly doubled from 422,000 nonprofits in 1987 to 800,000 in 2005, providing people with many more options in making charitable contributions.[9] Yet academic institutions and music libraries have a definite advantage in attracting donations because of the loyalty they establish with their alumni. Donors often formulate their giving decisions based on personal affiliations to an institution or certain causes in which they strongly believe. As executive director of the Queens Library Foundation, Jamaica, New York, Stanley E. Gornish observes, "There will be a direct correlation between your effectiveness in raising money for your library and your ability to convey a certain 'status' to a prospect that money alone can't. It is this status of being part of a select group and the feeling of positive power in doing something worthwhile for a worthwhile institution that fuels the aspirations of the donor. It should underlie every fundraising action you take."[10] Using this academic connection to your favor will give the music library a distinct advantage in competing for fundraising dollars.

Websites and Blogs

With all of these considerations in mind, how do you appeal to potential donors so that they will want to contribute to your library? One obvious approach is to make use of the internet. Most libraries have websites in which they provide information about the library, collection, services, and staff. Many of these websites have specific news links that give readers the latest updates on library activities. A great deal of information is accessible with photographs, audio, and video all enhancing the online experience. Some libraries also include blogs to present the latest news. Readers can leave comments on some library blogs in order to increase two-way communication. RSS feeds can also automatically update users with news. Such a presentation of practical information through the website is helpful—even essential—to active users of a library.

While blogs and webpages are an excellent way to publicize a library's services, they are not necessarily the best approach to communicating with potential donors, most of whom are alumni. These individuals probably do not care about the daily activities and happenings of the library. They may not want to receive constant library updates online. Less frequent notification with a broader brush is usually more appropriate for these people. There are also generational differences to consider. Older alumni, who are often a library's major donors, do not expect the instant news demanded by younger people, nor do they use electronic resources to the extent of more recent generations.[11]

Newsletters

One proven vehicle for cultivating donors and informing users about library activities on a periodic basis is the library newsletter. When compared to the immediacy of blogs, newsletters may appear to be outmoded and static.[12] It is clear, however, that newsletters and blogs serve different purposes and that they can live happily together side by side. Newsletters serve various functions.[13] An occasional newsletter (issued once or twice a year) will summarize library activities for those people on your mailing list as well as members of the university community. For fundraising purposes, a newsletter provides an opportunity to promote the library while also mentioning recently received donations and the positive influence they have had upon the library. It is wise to list the names of all recent donors in each newsletter. Most donors enjoy seeing their names in print, and other potential supporters may be inspired to contribute after recognizing names on the list. (See "Stewardship" for more details on recognizing donors.) Newsletter articles written about large donations further promote the ways in which the library makes use of these gifts.

The library can produce a newsletter of varying lengths, in paper and electronic formats. Online newsletters tend to be shorter in size since links to websites can be presented as imbedded hyperlinks. Issuing a paper version of a newsletter may seem outdated because of the expense involved with printing, addressing, and mailing. It is also not the most "green" method of communication. The decision to issue a print or online newsletter will depend upon the intended audience. Many librarians today feel that the print library newsletter is better served in an online version. In discussing their library's print newsletter, Anthony J. Frisby, Daniel G. Kipnis, and Elizabeth G. Mikita of the Scott Memorial Library at Thomas Jefferson University commented: "The Library's newsletter likely suffered the fate of most other print communications—destined to sit in a mail pile on someone's desk until it got so old that the stack was simply discarded."[14] In examining the shift from print to online newsletters, a 2004 library survey of 264 colleges and universities (with 169 responses listed in *The Carnegie Classification of Institutions of Higher Education* as master's colleges and universities) revealed that 36 percent of libraries published an online newsletter.[15] However, online newsletters may not always receive as much attention as their print counterparts once gathered. The "lack of response from audience" more than doubled from 11 percent in a 1989 survey of print newsletters to 24 percent for online newsletters in the 2004 library survey just mentioned.[16] One of the major drawbacks is that readers can delete online newsletters instantly without examining the content.

The paper newsletter mailed to a donor may have a greater impact than an electronic version, especially when targeting a select audience that expresses interest in the library.[17] As fundraising author Kim Klein points out, "Some organizations simply post their paper newsletter on their Web site. Other organizations have done away with paper newsletters altogether and only send e-newsletters. Neither of these decisions is proving to be wise. E-newsletters and paper newsletters are actually quite different. . . . Having only an e-newsletter can decrease your visibility to donors, since that kind of newsletter is far too easily deleted from a long list of e-mail."[18] Print newsletters also serve as an effective handout during library events or tours, and the library can furnish them to development officers for distribution to prospects.

Because a newsletter represents your library, it should look professional, be free of errors, and include content that will invite readers to take a look. The unintentional omission of a recent donor's name can lead to bad feelings and possibly lost donations in the future. Always show a draft of the newsletter to the development office and library administration before mailing it out. The names of people on your newsletter mailing list may need approval as well. The downside to creating newsletters is the vast amount of time they take to write, edit, distribute, and print (for paper versions). Even a brief newsletter can involve much more staff time than one might assume. But the library should also consider the potential benefits in cultivating donors. The time put into such a project can be justified if it results in sufficient funding for the library.

A search of the internet reveals that some music libraries have a "news" section or blog on their library homepages rather than a formal newsletter. In this way, libraries can update news at any time. Not many music libraries issue a separate newsletter, either online or paper. They often feel that the time to produce a newsletter does not justify the effort. Only a few music libraries still issue their own paper newsletters, and that number is dwindling. The Eastman School of Music's *Sibley Muse* is representative of this trend. Begun in 1977, this paper newsletter was discontinued in 2008 in favor of an online news blog.[19] Producing a paper newsletter today can be defended if it helps to raise enough money or steward donors. One such example is the *High Notes* newsletter issued by Western Washington University's Friends of the Music Library.[20] This newsletter appears online and is distributed in about 350 paper copies.[21] *High Notes* promotes library fundraising events and serves as a fundraising vehicle. According to Western Washington University Music Librarian Marian Ritter, "Everyone is thrilled to be recognized in the newsletter for their gifts, and this stimulates more donations."[22] A form in this newsletter for renewing Friends' memberships also "generates considerable revenue" for the library.[23]

Another newsletter aimed especially at donors is *What's the Score?*, produced by the Lewis Music Library at MIT.[24] Issued twice a year, this paper and online newsletter serves the dual purpose of updating its audience about library news while also attracting donations. Short articles highlight library news and noteworthy gifts. The newsletter also lists every recent donor. Donations to the library have increased significantly in response to this newsletter. While the production of *What's the Score?* and its distribution can be time consuming for the music library staff, the rewards pay off both in cultivating and stewarding donors and in the positive public relations that the newsletter generates.[25] From a fundraising viewpoint, it is best to issue newsletters in the late fall. Donors often send their donations at the end of the year for tax purposes, and your newsletter might prompt them to think of your library when remembering their favorite charities. If possible, try to include a reply envelope. This convenience will most likely result in a larger number of donations.

In addition to music library newsletters, the university library, music department, and university as a whole may issue newsletters that are often outreach tools of the development office aimed at cultivating donors. Whether the music library publishes its own newsletter or not, see if news about the music library may appear in any of these publications. Submit articles that project a positive image about a vibrant and engaged music library. Donors are more likely to contribute to a successful library than to one that whines about a lack of funding and needed resources. As director of University Libraries at the University of Kentucky, Paul A. Willis commented about a library fundraising campaign at his institution: "I learned early in my fundraising experiences that pleading poverty and great need is rarely a good way to raise funds. Most donors view a program that is seriously underfunded as one of low institutional priory. Donors generally wish to make a strong program stronger, and even though the libraries had many weaknesses, they also had many strengths. It was the strengths that became the focus of the campaign."[26]

E-MAIL

While library newsletters can be a successful means of communication, do not overlook the power of e-mail. Some donors may prefer this method of communication, and it is certainly quicker and easier than the U.S. mail. E-mail is also effective when contacting many prospects at once. In 1992, MIT's Class of 1982 designated the Lewis Music Library as one of the fundraising areas on campus that it would support for its tenth reunion gift. Over the years, the library received relatively modest but loyal donations from some of these class members. As their twenty-fifth anniversary grew near, the music library contacted the small number of alumni library donors from that class who planned to attend the 2007 MIT commencement. An e-mail was sent to each person to acknowledge their previous library support and invite them to a music library open house on Commencement Day. There was no solicitation asking for donations; this was simply a way to cultivate and steward these alumni. Within a week of the e-mail, the library development office informed us that the music library had obtained several thousand dollars from a few of the 1982 graduates who had received e-mails from the library. This was a pleasant surprise and convincing proof of the immediate impact that e-mail can have when cultivating donors. (For more details about the Class of 1982 Music Library Fund, see appendix 1.)

OTHER NETWORK MEDIA

What about other online communication used for fundraising? Some college development offices create online flash presentations, consisting of slide shows with animation and audio, which they e-mail to targeted alumni. Individual academic departments often customize these presentations with the intent of inspiring and motivating alumni to donate money to their alma mater.[27] Fundraising videos and podcasts are also likely to become more prevalent in future years. Some music libraries are beginning to create podcasts and use YouTube for online publicity, and others will probably follow this trend in the future.[28] In addition, academic libraries are establishing their presence in social networking services such as Facebook,[29] MySpace, and

Twitter, as a way to publicize their services.[30] From a fundraising perspective, increasing numbers of potential donors are using such online resources and social networking to fulfill their informational needs. It is not unusual for donors to prefer a Facebook message to a phone call or e-mail.

Technology has dramatically changed the manner in which people contribute money today. Donors can just enter a mobile number into their cell phone to support a needy cause. Some websites allow buyers to make a donation to charities each time they make online purchases. This web use giving is referred to as "wugging" in internet lingo. Fundraising widgets and apps also make it easy for institutions to attract donors through mobile devices. A well-positioned "Donate Now" widget on a library's homepage or Facebook page could result in a welcome new source of donations. Growing numbers of fundraising apps are available for raising and donating money. One of the largest and most successful fundraising applications is Facebook's Causes, which started in 2007 and claims 150 million Causes members, 500,000 member-created causes, and $35 million raised for 27,000 nonprofits.[31] Such apps will most likely continue to attract more donors in coming years, and libraries will increasingly need to communicate through social networking and mobile technologies in order to reach its audience.[32] Potential donors will be lost if the library falls behind in this area. In spite of this trend, keep in mind that many of today's older and often wealthier donors may not relate to the social-network environment. Some of them still prefer print collections, paper letters, and phone calls. For the next few years, fundraisers will need to communicate in assorted ways to suit both analog and digital generations in order to obtain the maximum number of donors.

Personal Contact

When reminding people about your library and its needs, there is no substitute for personal contact. A short conversation can do more to establish a relationship than years of newsletters, written notes, podcasts, and e-mails. Of course, it is unrealistic to think that you will have time to talk to all of your donors. When an opportunity arises, however, take advantage of it. In corresponding with donors, invite them into the library for a tour or just to talk. Even a ten-minute visit can help you make a personal connection that lasts for years. If the donor has time, try to arrange a lunch or coffee after a library visit. Getting away from the library in this manner gives you an opportunity to get to know the donor on a more personal basis in a relaxed environment. Such informal meetings will no doubt strengthen your relationship with the donor. Also try to attend school concerts, events on campus, alumni activities and any other gathering that might attract people with an interest in the music library.

Major Donors

This discussion has centered on the cultivation of relatively minor donors, such as those who send a $25 or $200 check to the library once a year. Cultivating major prospects, however, requires a different approach when potential gifts are in the six-figure and million-dollar range.[33] Consider a scenario in which your development officer notifies you that your library has clearance to approach a major prospect in order to discuss a music library proposal. This opportunity could result in a high level of cultivation, especially if the development officer feels that this prospect shows genuine promise. Keep in mind that the development office will probably be initiating the work in this process. It could begin with telephone conversations between the development officer and the donor. The music librarian may or may not participate in these initial talks. If things look increasingly promising, the development staff will often arrange a personal meeting. The prospect might come to your school for a visit, or the development officer (and perhaps the librarian) will pay a visit to the prospect's home. This could mean flying across the country for one dinner. It may surprise you at how much funding the institution is willing to spend in these situations. The old saying, "you have to spend money to make money" really does hold true in the development world. These meetings will usually include some sort of direct solicitation for a donation.

In cultivating major donors, it is essential for the music librarian to clearly articulate those areas of the library that need funding. What is the goal of this fundraising? Why is it a compelling project? How will library users benefit? How will it be carried out, for how much money, and by whom? Is there a naming possibility for the library space, collections, staffing position, or other areas of need? One of the most effective ways of conveying a library's wishes is to write succinct proposals that delineate projects with their estimated costs. These proposals are referred to as "case statements."[34] Unlike grants to government agencies and private foundations, which can require exhaustive proposals with detailed budgets, effective case statements should remain brief and concise.[35] Many donors do not care to see too many specifics or even a detailed budget. At first, they just want to know the basics and the bottom line. If they take an interest in a proposal, the librarian can supply more details later.

In writing these proposals, the librarian should be careful to ask for sufficient funding to cover the project. The temptation is to make the project look attractive to the donor by requesting an unrealistically small budget. Underestimating the costs may increase the chances of receiving the donation, but you and your staff could suffer miserably if the donated money does not cover all the expenses. Put together a thorough and accurate budget even if a detailed one is not required. Check with your development officers to see what kind of proposal they prefer. Involve your staff and anyone else who may participate in such a project. Brainstorm ideas and get opinions on how to accomplish this work. Make sure that staff members in the music library and library administration buy into this proposal. When in doubt of costs, it is better to overestimate. The price of accomplishing projects is often higher than what you might first think. A donation should have a positive impact on the library and its staff, so be careful what you wish for. Librarians would be wise to write many case statements covering a variety of projects with a wide range of costs. The more possibilities, the more likely that one of these proposals will appeal to a donor.

Convincing the Library Administration and Development Staff

Thus far, we have examined the librarian's role in cultivating donors, especially alumni. The librarian should keep in mind that employees on campus need attention as well. As previously mentioned, you must promote the music library to your library administration and development staff. Remember too that the music library might be competing for funding with other libraries on campus and other departments within your institution. The music librarian needs to become a strong advocate who makes a persuasive case for causes that will benefit the library. The more confident and compelling the librarian's arguments, the better the chances are for success. Only by convincing the library administration and development office will the music library receive the backing it needs to pursue fundraising activities. Once the library receives a gift, it is responsible for spending the money wisely. With appropriate purchases and the successful completion of funded projects, the music library will gain greater credibility with its own institution in pursuing additional funding in the future.

SOLICITATION

Having identified a list of prospects and begun their cultivation, how does the music librarian contact them for money? Considering the strict stipulations established by development offices, the answer is: carefully, of course. This section of the book enters into the third step of the fundraising process commonly referred to as "solicitation." Asking people for money can be an intimidating and nerve-racking experience, especially for librarians not trained in this area. Even the term "solicitation" carries negative connotations, eliciting sleazy images that range from door-to-door salesmen to ladies of the night. For music library fundraising, we should consider the positive side of the process in which individuals have the opportunity to support projects that they strongly champion. Successful solicitation results in giving that is rewarding and fulfilling for the donor. The use of pressure or guilt for the sake of obtaining a donation is unacceptable. Donating should always be a pleasurable experience.

Passive Approach

There is a mantra in the development world that states, "You can't raise money unless you ask for it." Asking for money can occur in different ways. Librarians do not necessarily need to confront people directly in order to raise money. One effective method is the passive approach to solicitation in which the librarian sends out publicity, writes thank-you letters for donations, but rarely speaks directly to any donors.[36] The library publicizes the ways in which past donations have improved services, and how future gifts can address specific needs of the library. A compelling story is told in this way—so convincing, the library hopes, that it will motivate people to make a donation on their own. With proper cultivation and stewardship, such donors will become faithful contributors who steadily increase their giving over the years.

While major gifts attract the most attention, we should not overlook the cumulative effect of many modest but loyal donors. Donors' annual contributions of $25 can grow over the years to $500 then $1000 and more. Multiply a few of these gifts together, and you will see a significant impact upon the library budget. Although the literature on library fundraising often says to concentrate on soliciting major donors, do not underestimate the smaller donors. With patience and a minimum amount of stewardship, these seedlings can blossom over time. As Matthew Simon, senior consultant and principal at Tahoe Planning Professionals, Las Vegas, Nevada, observed:

> Million-dollar donors get big publicity, but unfortunately the average fundraiser does not meet many of them. . . . For most of us, successful fundraising is not measured by our ability to identify and reel in the big donor. Were that to be our benchmark, most of us would be miserable failures. Like workers who steadily save $100 per pay check toward a larger goal of a new house or a college education for the children, most fundraisers must set a goal and build incrementally toward the target, little by little.[37]

The library should not expect instant riches, but rather approach fundraising as a long-term investment. Patience is indeed a virtue when it comes to soliciting gifts.

Posting fundraising information on the web is a convenient method of passively approaching donors.[38] Some library websites and online newsletters appeal to donors by including a link that takes readers to an online donation form.[39] Advantages for establishing online giving links include: the creation of another giving location for donors, the ability to meet people's expectations for online convenience, the opportunity to attract new donors, and lower administrative costs.[40] Music library web pages occasionally feature a separate page that explains the benefits of giving as well as the types of gifts that the library accepts. See appendix 2 for a sample of various university music library donation web pages. Some websites are quite specific in their requests. The Royal College of Music Library lists particular needs with its "Restore a Score" program, which asks donors to give exact amounts of money for the preservation of certain scores (see appendix 2, fig. 10). Music libraries may not always receive permission to include such direct solicitation on their web page because the library's parent institution may prefer to list all donation information on one central website. The music library should at least inquire whether it may feature music donation information on its own homepage or include it on the institution's fundraising website. This type of advertising may solicit donations, but Adam Corson-Finnerty, Development and External Affairs, University of Pennsylvania Library, contends that libraries should not expect to receive heavy traffic just by putting up donation links on their websites. He suggests ways in which library websites should "pull" people into their sites with enticing attractions, while also "pushing" messages out to users.[41]

Telephone Solicitation

What about more active solicitation in which immediate results are the goal? One direct method of asking for donations is through telephone solicitation. Such an approach is not for the faint of heart; in fact, a thick skin will come in handy for this kind of work. In spite of its negative connotation, the fundraising telethon is a proven method that can result in a greater response than direct mail.[42] Colleges often use telephone solicitation to ask their alumni for donations. Currently enrolled students sometimes make these phones calls, serving as inexpensive labor as well as non-threatening and appealing representatives from the school. This method incorporates some degree of guilt, as those of us who receive such calls can testify. It can be more difficult to say "no" to an innocent young student than to a seasoned fundraising professional. One documented example of student calling for library support occurred at the Missouri State University Libraries, which established a successful telephone fundraising effort by having students contact parents of current students to request donations for the library collections. The university's development office had not been successful in contacting these parents, so it allowed the library to undertake this approach.[43] At least one music library has been brave enough to use telephone solicitation for fundraising. The Music Library at the University of Washington used volunteer students to call retired faculty and other potential donors. According to music librarian Judy Tsou, these efforts were moderately successful in obtaining donations for the library.[44] If a music library is interested in pursuing some type of telephone solicitation, contact the development office and alumni association in advance. With a targeted list of alums and donors and permission from the appropriate offices, this might be a successful method of raising funds.

One library system that showed true ingenuity in using the telephone to its advantage was the city of Vienna, Austria, which set up a "Library Erotica Hotline" as a fundraiser. For .39 euros per minute, callers could listen to Austrian actress Anne Bennent read hot passages taken from the city library's 300-year-old erotic fiction collection. Money raised from this inventive fundraiser went to the library's remodeling and expansion project.[45] Perhaps music libraries could follow suit and find faculty or library staff members to sing sultry songs and steamy arias all in the name of improving the library. If music libraries are interested in this approach, permissions within the university are especially recommended!

ANNUAL GIVING

Another way of soliciting donors is through the institution's annual giving program, often called the annual fund. Because of their frequency, annual funds usually pursue smaller donations. Solicitations occur through written letters, telephone calls, e-mails, and other forms of publicity. Annual funds are typically campus-wide development programs, although libraries may also run their own annual appeal for donations. In an attempt to increase their donor base, libraries sometimes ask to become part of an annual campus-wide fund drive by listing the library as one of several possible giving opportunities presented to donors. Of course, there may be competition for such exposure with academic departments also looking for their piece of the fundraising pie.

An additional tactic for libraries wishing to attract new donors is to request permission from the alumni/development office to contact alumni who have never contributed to an annual fund. Although these nondonors are considered the least promising prospects, approaching them is a place to start. With patience and proper cultivation, the library can develop valuable donors in this way.[46] A further creative approach is a "second ask" campaign in which the university library contacts all campus-wide annual fund donors to make a second donation, this time to the library.[47] Libraries might also want to join forces with library friends organizations that have annual fund drives to solicit donations and new members. Annual fund drives often target reunion classes as another justification for approaching alumni. In order to attract new donors to libraries, well-known campus figures such as college athletic coaches may even spearhead a library's annual fund or capital campaign.[48] Music librarians should check with their development officers to see how the music library fits into the college library or campus-wide annual fund appeals.

Capital Campaigns

While the annual giving effort makes a broad appeal in search of many smaller donations, a capital campaign seeks major gifts from a more select pool of donors. Institutions go through cycles of major fundraising efforts called capital campaigns in which they establish a specific amount of money as the target goal.[49] These campaigns take place during a set period of time, generally over several years. Capital campaigns often raise money in the millions and even billions. Because of the dollars involved, the development office may hire additional staff members specifically for the campaign. Capital campaigns consist of well-planned strategies with certain timetables and tactical methods of approaching donors according to their giving capacities. The institution publicizes projects in need of funding to alumni in order to create interest and attract donations. Senior administrators set priorities for funding based on fundraising proposals received throughout the campus. The library director may be part of these discussions. If possible, the music library should make its needs known as well. Establishing a music library project as a priority in a capital campaign would be a major accomplishment.

Alumni

The college's alumni association may also provide opportunities for solicitation, such as an alumni web page, newsletter, or fundraising phonathon. Check with your development representative about promoting the music library in any of those places. If alumni association staff members agree to this, provide them with as much literature as possible about the library and its needs, including a fundraising wish list. This information will increase the chances of a match being made between library and alumni. Some university libraries solicit parents of graduating students for donations to purchase books in honor of their child's graduation. Such programs connect the library to parents and new alumni, providing the library with potential prospects for the future.

"The Ask"

When the music library receives donations, the development office will analyze the donors and decide whether they should assign them a prospect manager. Most small donors will not have a ranking high enough to warrant such an assignment. If the interests and giving capacity of a donor match a library fundraising proposal, development officers may cultivate donors until they feel that a solicitation is appropriate. They may present donors with one or several proposals, frequently in the form of case statements, which can be customized to the donor's specific interests. After the donor considers these proposals, the development person will ask for a contribution, if the donor seems ready. The development field refers to this request as "the ask." Having been trained in the proper techniques of approaching people for money, development officers will probably prefer to do the asking themselves without help from the library staff. They solicit specific amounts of money in line with the prospect's giving potential. Asking people for this kind of donation is something that most librarians are not eager to do, and development workers are usually aware of this fact.[50] "The ask" may result in complicated questions from the donor involving tax laws or university policies. The development staff will need to negotiate these technical details carefully. With millions of dollars possibly at stake in a discussion, you can be sure that the right development staff will be there to help seal the deal. Asking for donations in this manner only comes after development officers have done their homework and have properly prepared the donors for this moment. The prospect is usually well aware that "the ask" is coming.

One final point to remember: a librarian should never (ever, ever!) ask anyone for a donation unless permission has been cleared by the development office. The development world has this strict regulation in order to present a united and controlled approach to solicitation. Without such structure, various people on campus could contact prospects at any time for whatever amount of money. For example, three different university people might ask a major donor for $5,000,000, $500,000, and $5,000. This situation would be confusing to the donor and detrimental to the university, especially if the prospect decides to give just $5,000 because that request came first. There is just reason for strict hierarchical control of solicitation. One improper "ask" by the music librarian could tarnish and seriously impair his or her relationship with the development office.

Donor Expectations

During the solicitation process, the music librarian works hard to engage donors with the library. Unfortunately, an occasional donor may become too involved. These donors pay excessive attention to details, feeling entitled to control their donation rather than trusting the library to oversee it. They may recommend (or worse, demand) specific titles or composers to collect, suggest certain music-notation software to purchase, or propose what color carpet to acquire. They might try to take advantage of their donor status by asking for special library privileges as well. Given the amount of time and energy these donors can absorb, their involvement can actually be detrimental to the library. Library staff can spend endless hours trying to accommodate their requests. Even more discouraging is that these donors do not always improve over time. Their controlling habits can continue as long as the library staff yields to their demands. Ironically, the amount of money contributed is not always a factor. Donors of relatively modest gifts may also be the most demanding ones. If the library recognizes such donors before they commit to a donation, it should negotiate the terms of the donation and carefully document the library's and donor's expectations in the formal gift agreement to protect the library. If the donor and library cannot agree, the library should consider rejecting the gift. This decision is often best for the library in the long run. Remember that fundraising should always be a positive experience for the donor as well as the library. A donor whose expectations are not met will likely be unhappy. A despondent donor, particularly one who is well connected or who verbalizes frustrations, can damage the library's fundraising success overall.

STEWARDSHIP

After the library receives a donation, the librarian's work with the donor is far from over. Now comes the fourth stage of donor relations: stewardship. Stewardship refers to the contact that the librarian has with a donor after receiving a gift. Proper stewardship requires that the librarian keep the donor informed about the ways in which the donor's gift is benefiting the library and, over time, it will help to strengthen the donor's relationship with the library. Unfortunately, it is easy to neglect stewardship. After experiencing the initial excitement and satisfaction of receiving a donation, the library staff may feel that their work with the donor is done. The library accomplished its fundraising work, which probably took considerable effort, so why not send a quick thank-you note, spend the money, and go on to the next donor? First, the donor deserves the library's gratitude and appreciation. This is simply good manners. Also important from a fundraising position, donors have the potential to give the library even more. As fundraising professionals know very well, current donors are the most likely candidates for future contributions. After giving to the music library, many donors feel a certain commitment to you and your library. You will want to deepen and enrich this bond with the donor. The relationship should be ongoing.

Formal Thanks

Upon receiving a donation, what is the first thing to do? Just ask any parent whose children receive stacks of presents at their birthday parties. Write those thank-you notes! One of the most essential responsibilities of a librarian raising funds is to thank the donor. Why is this so important? Imagine the following scenario: A wealthy alumnus decides to show his appreciation to the three universities that he attended. Having spent a great deal of time in the music libraries at each school, he sends $250 to each. The first music library never sends him a reply. Because he finally receives his cancelled check, he knows that the library obtained the gift. After two months, the second library sends him an acknowledgement form letter signed by the university library director. Within two weeks, he receives a personal letter from the music librarian at the third library in which the librarian tells him how much the gift means to the library and even describes some of the ways in which the gift will be spent. The next year, the donor again brings out his checkbook. Instead of writing three checks, he decides to write just one check for $750 this year. You can probably guess which music library will be receiving that check. This example may seem obvious but it reminds us that thank-you letters can change the way in which people respond to giving. Keep in mind, too, that letter writing is becoming something of a lost art. When people receive a personal letter in the U.S. mail, they may especially appreciate that individual touch.

Some development professionals recommend that major donors be thanked not just once, but as many as seven times per gift.[51] Such thanks can come in the form of letters, telephone calls, e-mails, acknowledgements in newsletters, invitations to library events, small gifts from the library, and the naming of rooms or entire libraries for large donors. While keeping a running scorecard of the number of thanks sent to a donor may not be feasible for most, the point is that you cannot thank a donor too many times. Most donors appreciate the recognition. Some individuals like public acknowledgement while others prefer private thanks and even anonymous designations. As you get to know your donors, you will need to adjust the method of thanking them accordingly. For major donors, the types of thanks will differ significantly from smaller donors. Thank-you letters for exceptional gifts should be sent not only from the music library but also from upper university administrators, even the school's president. If possible, recruit music faculty members and students who benefit from donations to write letters or send e-mails that you can forward to major donors. Donors especially enjoy hearing from those individuals whose work has been positively influenced by their gift. For smaller donors, a personal thank-you note from the music librarian and an acknowledgment in a library newsletter (if one is issued) should suffice. The development office and the university library director often mail their own letters acknowledging gifts as well.

What makes a good thank-you letter? If possible, express your thanks through a paper letter or card delivered in the U.S. mail. An e-mail message may be sent in conjunction with a snail mail letter, but it does not take the place of the paper version. In composing letters, librarians should write in a concise, clear manner but also in a style that feels comfortable and genuine. Most thank-you letters should be just one page. Saying "thank you" at the beginning and end of the letter is a basic yet effective approach. Some fundraising resources recommend that the pronoun "you" should appear frequently in fundraising letters.[52] However, you should not attempt to adopt formulas that may sound insincere or contrived. Tell the donor how you plan to spend the money in general terms such as purchasing music scores or CDs. This approach reassures the donor that you are spending the money directly on items that will benefit the library. Remind the donor that his or her gift—even if it is small—has a real impact on your library. If you are acquainted with the donor, try to personalize the letter. Mention a conversation or experience that you both shared, or discuss a donor's favorite composer or recording artist in order to give the letter a less formal and more personal touch. The letter's message should state clearly that a gift to the music library is going to directly benefit many people, and that the donor will not be forgotten. Do not, as some mail order professionals suggest, ask for more donations in a thank-you note.[53] Such aggressive tactics would be inappropriate in an academic setting.[54] You may want to send copies of thank-you letters to your development officers so that they can keep track of the correspondence. Their expertise in letter writing may also provide you with some hints on composing better and more convincing letters. For gifts from donors with prospect managers assigned, it is wise to share drafts of your letters with them prior to mailing.

Music libraries will receive donations in many shapes and sizes. Thank-you letters should be sent for all donations, from the $500,000 donation to the $10 check or yet another copy of Hanon exercises. You want to show your appreciation and continue the possibility of future donations. When you begin to build up your donor pool, you will have more and more thank-you letters to write. This is not a trivial amount of work. Letter writing can take considerable time especially if you personalize each letter. One time-saving approach is to send the same basic letter to all small donors. Donors of any amount, however, do not appreciate receiving form letters. Form letters or even an improper signature can upset donors. Consider a Houston organization that sent out its thank-you notes late one year with a signature by the secretary rather than the company's director. The next year, the annual fund drive received less than half its normal contributions because donors felt that they had not been properly recognized.[55]

A compromise to writing one form letter for all gifts is to compose several form letters, each one thanking for a specific category of donations. For instance, you might compose one letter for small cash donations to the library, another for specific endowment funds, and still another for gifts in kind, and so forth. Save these letters on file and you can mail them out quickly, addressing each individual personally. By using form letters in this manner, the library will need to compose just a few letters for several donors. Since most donors contribute no more than once a year, it should suffice to update and revise these letters annually. If you receive more than one donation from a donor within a year, take the time to send a revised letter with up-to-date news. Be sure to sign each letter individually, preferably in blue ink, to show that you actually signed rather than just photocopied the letter.

Some librarians may prefer to send handwritten notes. If your volume of thank-you letters is high, such handwritten notes can become time consuming. A handwritten note, however, is an especially personal way to communicate. Handwritten notes are also appropriate to mark major life occasions such as a birth, death, or wedding. Such notes would probably be sent only to those major donors with whom the librarian has an especially close relationship. For librarians without the time for a handwritten note, a few words handwritten in ink at the bottom of a printed letter can also reach out to the donor in a personal way. Just the words, "Many thanks, John!" or "Thanks, Mary. We always appreciate your help!" will show that the librarian is thinking of the donor and not just blindly signing form letters. Personalizing letters and notes can go a long way in building donor loyalty.[56]

Once the letter is composed, the next rule of thumb is to mail it out as quickly as possible. A timeline recommended in many development circles is to send your response within forty-eight hours of receiving the donation,[57] or as some fundraisers put it, "thank before you bank."[58] This is an admirable goal, but for those workers in busy music libraries, it is not always a realistic one. For example, many donors make their contributions at the end of the year for tax purposes. Because late December may coincide with final-exam week and holiday vacation times, sending out thank-you letters may be difficult or impossible. If you fail the forty-eight-hour rule, there is no need to stress over it. Just do not wait several weeks before sending a response.

Prompt Communication with Central Development

The topic of timely acknowledgements relates to the potential issue of how quickly a library receives notification of donations. Sometimes donors will mail checks directly to the music library. Often, however, donors will send checks or donations electronically to the university's central development office or to the school's alumni association office where they may sit for some time before the library learns about the gift. Nothing can be more damaging to a donor relationship than a gift that goes unacknowledged for weeks or even months. This oversight is especially embarrassing if you have a local donor who visits your library. If there is no sign of appreciation from the library staff, the donor may view the staff as ungrateful and wonder if the gift was too small to elicit a verbal acknowledgement. Prompt and clear communications between the offices receiving donations and the library will help to alleviate misunderstandings and potentially awkward situations.

Tours

Another way to thank a donor, as previously mentioned under cultivation, is to offer private tours of the music library. Behind-the-scenes tours are attractive activities for local donors, or donors returning to campus, and will give them an opportunity to get to know you and your library better. Donors will come away with a fuller understanding of the benefits that the music library provides and they will feel a stronger connection that could lead to future support.[59] During tours, point out how previous donations have contributed to the library's improvement. When stewarding larger donors, invite selected music faculty members to join you so that they can not only express their appreciation but also explain how the donor's gift is assisting their specific teaching and research needs. People like to contribute to a successful operation but they also want their donation to be spent wisely. One survey reveals that over 80 percent of donors indicate that a library's efficient and effective use of donations is a major consideration in making their philanthropic decisions.[60]

Bookplating

Bookplates are a time-honored way to acknowledge and steward donors. Affixed to the inside cover of library materials, such as a book or score, bookplates recognize the individual who is responsible for obtaining particular library items. Bookplates can range in style from the simple typing of a donor's name on a plain label to elaborate designs, some of which are commissioned works of art.[61] Large endowed collection funds are especially appropriate for custom-designed bookplates. To prevent surprises, let donors have the opportunity to provide the wording and, possibly, the design of their bookplates. Bookplates provide an excellent means of visibly acknowledging a gift while also serving as a reminder of its lasting value to the library. Such an enduring quality is especially appropriate and comforting for those individuals giving memorial gifts. One attractive yet inexpensive way to acknowledge generous donors is to mat their bookplate in an attractive frame and present it to them as a gift. Because of the cost to design and process bookplates, the library will probably require a minimum monetary donation before it produces customized bookplates for that gift.

Expenses to maintain a bookplate program have led some libraries to eliminate paper bookplates altogether in favor of electronic bookplates that appear within online library catalog records. In this way, the library saves money and donors receive recognition before a wider audience. Another advantage is that small physical materials, such as CDs and DVDs, that cannot accommodate a paper bookplate can now receive electronic acknowledgement, as can digital-only items such as e-books. Older donors and librarians may yearn for the physical bookplate, but its electronic version will no doubt increase in libraries over the coming years. The trend toward more electronic books and online resources will also decrease the demand for paper bookplates.

ONGOING EXPRESSIONS OF THANKS

After these immediate expressions of appreciation, major donors should receive additional periodic thanks in the future. Thanking these donors can be as simple as an occasional telephone call. This kind of follow-up may sound obvious but it is easy to put off. Most librarians get caught up in daily work. Years may come and go before they contact a donor. The phone call does not need to be long or involved—just a "thinking of you" message in which the librarian tells donors how their money has been spent and what it means to the library. Do not underestimate how much a phone call can delight a donor, especially if the call comes a few months after the initial excitement about the gift has quieted down. Telephone calls are especially welcomed by retired individuals who are often easy to reach at home and who are frequently more than happy to talk. If your donor is still actively working and has a busy schedule, you might consider an occasional e-mail. When this approach produces a quick response to your message, make a note that future e-mails are in order. Younger donors may relate to a message through Facebook or other social media. Try to customize your communication approach according to donors' lifestyles. Be sure to contact donors periodically; write the dates of future phone calls or e-mails in a long-term calendar. Consult your development officer about the types of communication you may pursue. Certain methods could be off limits. Random telephone calls from librarians to donors might frighten development staff, and the possibility that such conversations could result in librarians asking for money or negotiating legal contracts is bound to keep the development staff up at night. Once librarians prove that they understand the rules of development and that they are not loose cannons sailing among the campus's fundraising fleet, they should be given increasing freedom to communicate with donors.

Proper stewardship of donors requires significant staff time, especially as your donor pool expands. Keep in mind that stewardship is not just strategically wise from a fundraising standpoint, but is also the polite thing to do. Even if no future funding appears from a donor, you have made the effort to express the library's gratitude for someone's generosity. But chances are likely that you will receive additional donations if the library properly stewards the relationship with the donor. Do not overlook the significance of stewardship within the cycle of fundraising. It will be essential to the success of your fundraising efforts.

Chapter Three

TYPES OF DONATIONS

Individuals often seek out the music library as a place to send donations even if the library makes no fundraising efforts. Whether a library is actively seeking gifts or not, it should prepare to deal with them. Gifts can appear in many forms, such as a collection of 78-rpm opera recordings, a piece of popular sheet music, a long run of *The Etude*, or a cash gift supporting the library's jazz holdings. This chapter will examine the types of gifts a music library can expect to receive from donors.

GIFTS IN KIND

Perhaps the most common (as well as notorious) library donations are gifts in kind. This term refers to physical materials that a library receives. For music libraries, gifts in kind can encompass a wide range of materials, including books, journals, music scores, manuscripts, photographs, concert programs, and audio and video recordings in various formats. Other music-related materials, including musical instruments, artwork, and audiovisual equipment, may also be offered as gifts to music libraries. Gifts in kind come in two varieties: solicited and unsolicited.

SOLICITED GIFTS

Solicited gifts in kind are materials that a library actively pursues. Examples include a composer's manuscript collection or an individual's private library of rare books and scores. These gifts in kind can be the most precious donations that a library will ever receive—the librarian may spend years soliciting potential donors for valuable materials. Such collections can strengthen a library's holdings overnight and provide research materials as well as prestige to a library for generations to come. Since large research libraries, both academic and public, are more likely than smaller institutions to have the appropriate space and staffing, they are more apt to solicit and obtain prized collections.[1] Gifts in kind may be highly esteemed but they can also be expensive to process, catalog, and maintain. Grants and private contributions may be sought in order to pay for maintaining these materials.

UNSOLICITED GIFTS

Unsolicited gifts in kind, on the other hand, are not the gifts that you pursue, but rather those that pursue you. They come by way of phone calls or by simply appearing in a brown paper bag on the circulation desk. Sometimes such gifts take the form of musty, torn, or worm-eaten collections that will only waste staff time without any benefit to the library. It is this type of donation, unfortunately, that many librarians envision when they think of gifts in kind. Unsolicited gifts in kind are not always trash, however. They can sometimes present the library with much-needed items that help to fill lacunae in the collection. Screen gifts carefully before the library accepts them.[2] When a donor telephones the library to see if it will accept materials, the librarian should ask detailed questions about the collection. If the collection is large, make a trip to the person's home to view the materials when possible. Although time consuming, this trip may save you and your staff countless hours by eliminating unwanted items before they enter the library. Someone's description over the telephone can often differ dramatically from reality.

Librarians should be cautious to accept only those items that fit within the scope of their collection and that will add value to the library. Keep in mind the cost of processing, cataloging, and storing these materials. Obtaining materials may be free, but the actual cost of adding materials to the library can be much more expensive than the library staff realizes (see Chapter Six, "Hidden Costs"). Because of these costs, libraries can benefit from conducting cost-benefit analyses to determine if gifts in kind are worth the expense.[3] Depending upon a library's finances, the librarian might consider asking the donor if a monetary contribution could accompany the gift in kind to cover processing, preservation, and cataloging costs. Once donors learn about these expenses, they may be willing to contribute financially, especially if they are told that such funding will allow the library to process their materials in a timely fashion, rather than putting the donation in storage indefinitely—not a desirable option for either party involved.

Carefully check the condition of donated materials. If possible, open all newly donated items in an isolated room away from the library collection. Examine materials for signs of bugs, such as silverfish, ants, fleas, and worms. Even the finest collection will not be worth accepting if it brings the possibility of infesting the library. Similarly, reject any donation of materials covered with mold or mildew. The fact that items have been stored in someone's attic or basement should raise a red flag and suggests that a visit to the collection may be in order before the library accepts it.

Contracts

The library can protect itself by telling a donor that it accepts gifts in kind only under conditions established by the institution. Supplying the donor with a written contract that spells out an institution's gift policies will help to prevent any misunderstandings.[4] In working with significant gifts in kind, as well as monetary agreements such as endowments, planned giving, or major gifts, always consult your development officer, who will communicate with the institute's gift recording secretary and legal counsel in preparing these agreements/contracts. This will ensure clear documentation and agreed-upon use of the funds between donor and institution. Librarians should never negotiate such documents on their own. Leave it to the development professionals to conduct this work. Do not be afraid to reject gifts that will not enhance your library. Point to the library's collection development policy statement and gift policies in order to ensure would-be donors that the library bases its gift decisions upon these criteria rather than just personal whims of the staff.[5] On the library's website, post those materials that the library does not collect—such as 78-rpm recordings, eight-track tapes, or music magazines—in order to deter donors from making inappropriate contributions. Finally, be ready to suggest other libraries or venues that may be a better match for unwanted materials.

A benefit to accepting gifts in kind is the relationship that the library creates with the donor. Having contributed materials, the donor will sometimes develop stronger connections with you and your library. Additional gifts in kind and even monetary gifts may be forthcoming if the library stewards the donor properly. However, the librarian should avoid the temptation to accept otherwise unwanted gifts in kind just for the purpose of recruiting new donors. For more details about libraries accepting music gifts in kind, see the instructive article by Kristin Heath and Terra Merkey, which also provides examples of gift policies and forms.[6] Appendix 2 contains gift information on various music library websites.

Tax Deductions

A donor's inclination to make gifts, both monetary and gifts in kind, is sometimes to obtain tax credits from the Internal Revenue Service (IRS). With gifts in kind of any value, a donor needs to receive an acknowledgment letter from the library and to keep written records of the donated items. For gifts in kind, the donor generally uses the fair market value to determine his or her tax deduction.[7] The library should acknowledge the receipt of a gift in kind with "a reasonably detailed description of the property."[8] Most often a count of the number of items received (six compact discs, four books) is sufficient. Tax deductions for gifts in kind valued from $500 to $5,000 require donors to file IRS Form 8283 with their tax returns; for gifts in kind valued over $5,000, donors must obtain a written, professional appraisal indicating the material's fair market value in addition to filing IRS Form 8283.[9]

The library must not provide appraisals; doing so would be a conflict of interest. The donor is responsible for obtaining an independent appraisal at his or her own cost. A library accepting a gift in kind valued over $5,000 must fill out Part IV of IRS Form 8283 (Donee Acknowledgement). If the library sells or otherwise disposes of a gift in kind exceeding $5,000 within three years of receiving it, the library must notify the IRS (including the amount for which the object was sold), using IRS Form 8282, and also notify the donor.[10] While libraries may not conduct appraisals of any donations, they may provide donors with directories and lists of qualified appraisers to aid a donor in finding an appropriate appraiser.[11] To protect itself and the donor, a charity should never direct a donor to a specific appraiser in relation to a gift in kind but always provide several options. It is advisable to give donors a list of five or as many as ten professionals from which they can choose. If this is not possible, one can also advise the donor to check with a major auction house (and share a list of two or three from which they can choose). They are generally equipped to recommend several independent appraisers for specific types of materials. Of course, if a donor does not want a charitable tax deduction, no report to the IRS is necessary.

Librarians should be aware of such basic tax regulations that apply to donations. Tax laws governing charitable gifts that are established by the IRS can change from year to year, however, making it difficult for a music librarian to stay current with these laws.[12] Because of the complexity of tax regulations, it is best not to give any tax advice to a donor. Donors with questions concerning tax laws should always be referred to your university's development office or general counsel or else their lawyer or financial advisor.

MONETARY GIFTS

Whereas gifts in kind may or may not be wanted by the library, it is hard to imagine when monetary gifts would not be welcome. Cash gifts provide the funding needed to improve a library in ways that are not possible with a library's yearly budget. The library will place monetary donations in either restricted or unrestricted funds. Money in restricted funds purchases certain materials or supports specific projects that a donor usually designates. Unrestricted funds are available for the purchase of anything regardless of category. Donors often prefer restricted funds because they know where their money is going. However, if librarians have their choice, they will prefer an unrestricted fund because of the freedom it provides. Some institutions use the terms "endowed" for restricted and "expendable" for unrestricted funds.

Unfortunately, the amount of money a donor gives the library may not always be the amount that the library receives. Some university administrations take a percentage out of monetary gifts in order to defray university expenses. The percentage removed will vary from school to school, so ask your development staff if this rule applies at your institution.

One way to increase the size of donations is to remind donors that some companies and corporations support matching the amount of money that their employees give to a charitable organization. Matching gifts can double a donation without costing the donor any additional expense. Cash donations from individuals will arrive year-round, but the vast majority are usually sent in November and December as donors seek end-of-the-year tax write-offs or at the end of the university's fiscal year when campus fundraisers are actively pushing to receive gifts and drive up the university's annual fundraising totals.

One method of encouraging donors who are hesitant to contribute a large gift is to allow them to make payments through installments. A gift of $50,000 may seem imposing to a donor but five yearly payments of $10,000 may be more comfortable for one's budget. If reporting a cash donation to the IRS for a tax deduction, regardless of the amount, library donors must have a receipt or formal acknowledgement letter from the library or university indicating the date and amount of money received. Often, as part of gift processing, your university will send the donor a formal gift receipt. Before acknowledging gifts, be sure to check with your development office or university gift processing office to confirm whether they send tax receipts to all donors.

PLANNED GIVING

Libraries sometimes rely upon planned or deferred giving to obtain significant portions of peoples' estates. Estimates indicate that historically 80 percent of all endowment funds are a result of planned giving and bequests.[13] Such gifts can benefit the library immediately, but often the library will receive them sometime in the future, usually after the death of the donor. By making planned gifts to charitable nonprofit organizations, individuals can gain favorable tax benefits during their lifetime as well as removing taxable assets from their estates. Although such tax advantages may be appealing, they are not the only reason that donors contribute money. In fact, a National Committee on Planned Gifts study indicates that donors are motivated by the following reasons (in order of importance): an aspiration to support charities, the manner in which their gift will be used, tax benefits, and advantages to estate planning objectives.[14] Librarians should not expect planned gifts to come their way just because of tax reasons; they must also promote their library and its needs to potential donors as part of a total giving package.

While the basic concept of planned giving will be helpful for librarians to understand, extensive and up-to-the-minute knowledge in this area is not essential. When delving into this area of fundraising, librarians should rely on assistance from the development staff at their institutions. In fact, the university would not expect or want the music librarian to negotiate such complex legal documents. As Lisa Browar, university librarian at New School University, and Samuel A. Streit, associate university librarian for special collections at Brown University, point out:

> While librarians may encourage certain donors to consider various planned giving instruments as part of their personal long-term investment strategies or estate plans, no librarian should ever dispense estate planning advice or tax advice to a potential donor, nor should a librarian attempt to execute a planned giving instrument. Planned gifts can be exceptionally complicated instruments to construct and execute, and they require the services of lawyers, accountants, and other tax and estate planning professionals.[15]

With this in mind, the following discussion will mention a few of the better-known choices for planned giving.

Types of Planned Gifts

Planned gifts can be divided into three broad categories: bequests, life-income gifts, and other types of planned gifts.[16] The parent institution is the official recipient of these gifts, even though the library may be named as the area that receives the funding.

Bequests

Donors can make a bequest through their wills, in which some or all of their estate is left to the library. This is a common form of planned giving for libraries. Donors may bequeath anything of monetary value, such as cash, real estate, securities, or objects of value to the library. Donors may specify an amount of money or property, or they may leave the library a percentage of their estate. Donors retain possession of the bequeathed donation until their death, and bequests are revocable (that is, donors can change them during their lifetimes). Ideally, the donor will inform the institution or library of the bequest while they are alive and discuss with the library staff how the library will use this donation.

Life-Income Gifts

Life-income gifts are irrevocable (not changeable) vehicles for transferring funds from an individual's financial portfolio to the institution while the donor is alive. These types of gifts take the form of annuities and trusts. Such agreements can provide donors with considerable savings in capital gains, income taxes, and estate taxes.

The charitable gift annuity is a contract that allows an individual to donate assets to a designated institution. In return, the institution pays the individual a fixed amount of money per year (a set percentage of the initial gift, agreed upon at the time of the gift) for the length of the person's life. Upon the individual's death, the college retains the principal. A deferred charitable gift annuity usually attracts younger donors who do not currently need the income from their savings. By making this gift, donors obtain immediate tax credit and receive annual payments from the college at a later time, often at retirement, for the rest of their lives.

A charitable remainder trust is a method for donors to place assets into a trust in which they designate themselves (or possibly other beneficiaries) to receive a certain income for their lifetime or for a certain number of years. Different types of charitable remainder trusts are possible. The two most common trusts are the charitable remainder annuity trust (CRAT), which pays a fixed percentage of the initial gift for the life of the trust, and the charitable remainder unitrust (CRUT), which pays a fixed percentage of the trust's value as assessed each year.

A pooled income fund is another type of life-income gift, in which several donors contribute to one large conglomeration of money and receive a set amount of income. The donor's share of the pooled fund is withdrawn from the pool and distributed to the college upon the donor's death. There are varying tax benefits for each kind of planned gift. The university planning giving officer should always be consulted before discussing any life income gift (trust) with a donor.

Other Types of Planned Gifts

Less common planned giving vehicles include charitable lead trusts in which the institution receives a percentage of the principal for a period of time, but the institution does not retain the principal. At the end of the defined lead period, the principal transfers to the donor or a designated beneficiary. In this way, the donor assists the library for a period of time but then transfers the wealth to designated individuals, thus minimizing or avoiding certain taxes. Another giving option is life insurance. Individuals may designate the institution as beneficiary.

In all of these methods of planned giving, donors and or their estates can receive substantial tax relief in addition to the satisfaction of leaving their legacy in support of a library.[17] Planned gifts that the library negotiates today usually do not provide an immediate benefit. In fact, the librarians and development staff that help create such legal documents may or may not work or even live long enough to see these agreements come to fruition. Librarians should keep a long-term perspective, however, and realize the significant impact that these gifts will have on future generations. Music librarians decades from now will be thankful for the visionary work that we accomplish today with planned giving.

ONE-TIME DONATIONS FOR SPECIAL PROJECTS

While planned giving will meet the needs of some donors, others may be willing to contribute a major amount of money to be spent immediately. Music libraries should make their wishes known to the development office, especially for large-scale projects such as new building construction, renovations, improved equipment and furniture, new staffing, or other major enhancements. Money to support these projects can be spent quickly. For various reasons, including tax benefits, a one-time expenditure may attract a donor. A one-time donation can fulfill an urgent need for the library while showing immediate and tangible results to the donor.

Naming Opportunities

One way to attract major donors is to provide naming opportunities within the library. The naming of rooms, sections of the library, or the entire library is a customary method for acknowledging donors. A naming opportunity provides an enduring legacy to the donor and a certain sense of immortality that can appeal to some individuals. Check with your development office to see what stipulations the university has established for naming opportunities. The university usually establishes a range of monetary levels to support different naming categories. Because these are major contributions, the development staff will most likely negotiate the naming rights and "prices" with the donor. Consult with development staff members about potential naming opportunities so that they will keep your library in mind when talking to major prospects.

ENDOWMENTS

Some donors may prefer to make a donation that will keep giving over the years. That is the attraction of an endowed fund. Endowments invest a donor's money so that a portion of the interest of the fund is paid out each year in perpetuity to be used by the library. The principal remains invested and untouched. Such donations are truly living legacies. Most libraries require a minimum donation to create an endowment in order to receive a sufficient yearly payment and justify the university's expense managing the endowment. The original donor and others can continue to add money to the fund to increase its buying power. If the institution invests the endowment money properly, the principal and the interest will grow over the years.

Money invested in a library endowment is usually managed by a financial office within the university. The library will receive just a small percentage of the total endowment value, depending upon current interest rates and financial market returns as well as university administrative costs. The annual return to the library will fluctuate over time. Endowments need substantial funding to produce an annual disbursement of significance. To earn enough interest to cover the annual salary for a staff position, for example, an endowment fund would need to be in the millions of dollars. Endowments are also a nice way to honor someone with a memorial gift. Friends and relatives of the honoree can take pride and comfort in contributing to such a fund.

ENDOWMENTS TO SUPPORT COLLECTIONS

Endowments support a library in a variety of ways. One prevalent type, the collection endowment, helps to sustain and develop a library's collection. Collection endowments, also referred to as "book" or "information-resource" endowments, are not just for books. Music libraries offer other possibilities for endowments, including the acquisition of music scores and sound recordings. Endowments for scores especially appeal to donors, because, unlike the ever-changing formats of sound recordings, scores consist of a venerable format that should remain in the library for years to come. Donors with an appreciation for the online world may want their endowment to purchase subscriptions to electronic bibliographic databases or online streaming audio and video.

Restricted vs. Unrestricted Endowments

Some libraries allow donors to choose the subject areas that their collection endowment money will support. Donors' choices, unfortunately, do not always match the library's priorities. Libraries sometimes solve this problem by providing donors with a pre-selected list of acceptable subject areas, thus ensuring the library of funding for topics that need strengthening.[18] Other libraries make no such restrictions on the donor's choices, allowing the staff to negotiate terms as best it can. There are unfortunate examples of well-intended donors who insisted on choosing a subject or format so narrow that the library could not spend the yearly endowment in later years. An endowment from the 1920s that agreed to purchase only 78-rpm recordings or just foxtrot music would be difficult to fulfill today. To avoid this situation, libraries may want to encourage donations for unrestricted endowment funds so that money can be spent no matter what new technologies or musical styles appear in the future. However, such a fund might discourage donors with specific wishes and result in less money being raised.[19] In working with donors, the music librarian should remember that the purpose of a donation is to improve the library. If a donor's demands make the staff uncomfortable in any way, the music librarian should renegotiate and possibly reject the money. There is no reason to establish an endowment or accept any gift unless it will benefit the library both today and in the future. Librarians should work with the university development office to document endowment gifts, which generally involve the execution of a legally binding contract.

Donor Involvement

Libraries sometimes provide donors with a list of the titles purchased through their collection endowments. Although requiring extra work, this method of stewardship keeps the donor actively involved with the library. On the other hand, this kind of involvement can also cause its share of problems. Donors will sometimes question individual titles that do not suit their personal tastes and may begin to dictate the selection process. Librarians who prefer to select materials without any restrictions may resent such influence from a donor. They can avoid this controversy by sending donors just a selection of titles, or no titles at all. The problem of "helicopter donors" lessens if the collection endowment clearly stipulates the library's autonomy in selecting materials. Being upfront with the donor before a gift is made could save you trouble in the future. In some rare cases, donors have been known to demand their donations back from the university after disagreements arise concerning the use of a donor's money and influence over the university.[20]

Pooled Endowments

The minimum amount of money required to establish a library collection endowment will vary from school to school. Some libraries encourage smaller donations by creating "pooled endowments." This type of endowment allows donors to contribute smaller amounts of money to one common endowed fund that is set up for a specific purpose. Easier than obtaining one large donation, several smaller ones can be located faster and more readily.[21] Many smaller gifts, of course, make more work for the library and development office, which would prefer one large donation. However, the library has little control over the gift amounts that make donors comfortable. Regardless of their size, collection endowments appeal to both donors and librarians alike. These gifts can significantly broaden and strengthen a library's holdings over time.

Endowments for Staffing and Other Purposes

Besides collection endowments, academic libraries also create endowed funds to support a wide range of needs, from general operating costs to new staffing.[22] An example of an endowment for an eminent music library staff position occurred in 1998 when Harvard alumnus Richard F. French endowed the position of music librarian for Harvard University's Eda Kuhn Loeb Music Library. This was the first endowed music library chair in the country.[23] Endowments like this one are difficult to obtain because they lack the tangible attraction of collection endowments. It takes extensive education to convince prospects about the subtle but very real value of an endowed fund that supports staffing.

Chapter Four

FUNDRAISING EVENTS IN A MUSIC LIBRARY AND ELSEWHERE

There are many kinds of events with donors that can raise money for a music library, ranging from elaborate invitation-only settings to low-budget informal occasions open to all.[1] Before choosing an event, however, the library should clarify its fundraising goals. Is this event intended to raise money immediately or is it a free event that publicizes the library? Not all library events need to charge admission in order to be successful from a development perspective. Free events provide a venue to increase user awareness of the library as well as an opportunity to identify, cultivate, and steward donors. For events that raise funds, be realistic about the actual monetary profits and do not assume that such events are necessarily the best way to supplement a library's budget. Some professional fundraisers argue convincingly that fundraising events for nonprofit organizations are a poor use of staff time because of the expenses involved and the lack of justifiable payback to the sponsoring organization.[2] Nonetheless, the music librarian lacking patience to slowly cultivate prospects for the next twenty years may seek to generate some immediate cash through a library event. This chapter will examine the tempting world of library events and consider their viability as a fundraising source.

LIBRARY BENEFIT CONCERTS

Perhaps the most compelling event for a music library is the fundraising concert held in the library or another location. A music library can be an attractive setting for performances, especially if the music on the program comes from the library's collection. Because little is published about library benefit concerts, it is not easy to determine the full extent to which these concerts occur throughout the country. In 1995, Leonard Lehrman, president of the Long Island Composers Alliance, surveyed the topic of library concerts. Although he found little written about such concerts, he discussed some of the public and academic libraries that sponsored both free and fundraising concerts over the years. The Library of Congress still hosts a well-known and outstanding series of free concerts which began in 1925. As a local illustration, Lehrman pointed out that of the fifty-two public libraries in the Nassau Library System (western Long Island, New York) at least twenty-seven libraries owned grand pianos and five had uprights. Many of these libraries sponsored concert series. Lehrman suggested that mission statements of libraries should encourage concerts to be part of their outreach goals.[3]

Since the time of Lehrman's article, the published literature about library concerts remains sparse. A scan of the internet, however, reveals that these concerts take place quite frequently, especially in public libraries, which present both benefit and free concerts. Music concerts fit comfortably within the activities of public libraries, with their emphasis on outreach to the community. Academic music libraries, on the other hand, work with music departments that initiate their own concerts throughout the year. Concert giving is not usually within the domain of an academic music library, and fundraising through concerts often falls outside of a music librarian's job description. Therefore, creating a successful fundraising library concert at a university can be quite a challenge. While some books cover the general topic of organizing concerts, the following discussion examines aspects that relate specifically to music library benefit concerts.[4]

A few loyal library followers may attend a benefit concert just to support the library's cause, but you need to attract a wider audience in order to make the concert a financial success. The choice of performers will determine the amount of money that the library raises. People will pay high ticket prices to see well-known performers, but it is unlikely that they will spend much to watch students or music faculty perform unless they are celebrities.[5] Few libraries have the luxury of their own resident musical group—such as the Newberry Library's Newberry Consort—on hand to perform benefit concerts.[6] Some academic music departments and conservatories, however, feature artists of sufficient stature who could attract a vast paying audience, so the potential is there. Occasionally, an internationally renowned musician, such as violinist Anne-Sophie Mutter, will headline a library benefit concert, but that kind of blockbuster library benefit concert is rare.[7] If a music library has a connection with a major performing artist or ensemble, it might want to consider an ambitious benefit concert.

Before you decide to give Yo-Yo Ma a call, or even before speaking to students or faculty about performing for a benefit concert, first consider the amount of work involved in producing such an event. My own experience with benefit concerts began at the University of Missouri–Kansas City (UMKC) in 1988 and 1989.[8] These concerts, billed as "Encore Concerts," invited selected music alumni to perform light encore pieces in benefit of UMKC's Conservatory Library. A modest admissions fee was charged and the concerts took place in the conservatory's concert hall. Many people helped in the planning and implementation of this work, including the conservatory's library staff, faculty, library committee, alumni association, and the university's development office. While these concerts were successful and resulted in excellent publicity for the library, they lasted just two years. Unfortunately, the modest amount of money raised (in the hundreds rather than thousands) did not justify the hours of planning and preparation that went into these concerts. The mechanics of hosting a concert may seem simple enough, but in reality, can take an enormous amount of work. Here are just some of the factors to consider when organizing a library benefit concert:

Planning. The music library will need to create a proposal that clearly spells out the scope of the benefit concert and its goals. Early in the process, the library must determine who the administrative participants will be in this work. What roles go to the music library, university library, library friends group (if available), music department, development office, alumni office, publicity office, and others? The music library will need to coordinate many people in this effort.

Budget. What are the total anticipated costs? How much financial support and staffing will the other participating offices and departments on campus provide? How much money does the library need to raise in order to make a profit? Is the success of the concert based purely on the money raised or other intangibles such as publicity and goodwill?

Performers. Who will be the performers, and who will choose them? Will they be paid? If so, how much? If the performers are students, are they acceptable to the music department and its performance standards? The music department may want to rehearse these students to insure the quality of the performance. How many rehearsals will the performers need, if any? As previously mentioned, the fame of the performers will dictate the magnitude of the concert.

Music Selection. Who will choose the program? Is the music selected from the library collection or connected in any way to the library or the college? Does the music program have a particular theme? Will the library need to pay licensing fees for performing copyrighted music on the program?[9]

Admission Price. What admission price makes the most possible money without scaring people away? Will there be one ticket price or will prices vary according to seat location, student/senior discounts, and so forth? Is it best to have printed tickets? How will they be sold and distributed? In promoting ticket sales, the library should not announce that concert tickets are tax-deductible. The IRS does not allow a tax deduction for the purchase of concert tickets (or other items and services) unless someone pays more than the fair market value of the tickets. If people pay $50 for a $30 ticket, then they may deduct just $20 as a charitable contribution.[10]

Audience. What kind of audience will the library try to attract? Will it be open to the campus or a broader community?

Concert Date. During what time of the year will the concert occur? Consider schedule conflicts due to holidays and other events, along with the school calendar. Locating the right day of the week and time of day is essential in matching the character of the concert. For example, a noon concert on a weekday will attract a different audience from one held at 8:00 pm on a Saturday night.

Printed Concert Program. How fancy or simple is the printed program? Will a graphic artist design the program? How detailed are the program notes? Who will write them? Will vocal music include text of all the words? Who will write the biographies of the performers?

Location. What is the location of the concert? Will it be held in the library? If so, will the concert conflict with regular library hours? Will a piano be moved into the library? Will the concert be held in a music department performance hall or another location? Will there be a hall rental fee? Will there be a need for ushers and a stage manager?

Publicity. Publicizing the concert is essential for its success. Who will handle the promotion of the event? Will the publicity be campus wide, community wide, or re gional? Both pre- and post-concert publicity are necessary.

Photography. Will there be photographs of the concert and the people who attend? If so, will the library hire a photographer to capture the event? Who will organize and distribute the photographs?

Recording. Will someone record the concert to preserve it for the future and for publicity? If so, who will make the recording? Will it be an audio or video recording? If there are plans to broadcast or sell recordings of the concert, the performers and production staff will need to sign waiver forms for copyright purposes; it might be necessary to obtain licensing rights for the music.

Reception. Most benefit concerts require a reception after the performance. This provides an opportunity for people to socialize and meet the performers. The reception is also a time for the music library staff to thank people and to make new friends for the library. How extravagant or simple is the reception? Will caterers provide the food and drink? If alcohol is served, will the library need to follow special school regulations? Where will the reception take place? Will the library pay custodians to clean up after the reception?

Post-Concert Work. After the concert, the music library's work is not done. In addition to the tasks just mentioned, the library must write thank-you notes to all participants who helped with the concert. If anyone made contributions above the ticket price, the library should recognize those donors with written acknowledgments. The library will need to rectify and pay all expenses. Someone should write articles, blogs, and so forth to further publicize the event.

The list of activities above, while certainly not comprehensive, points out some of the planning and administration necessary for a successful fundraising concert. The list also gives an indication of the expenses. This description is not meant to discourage anyone from attempting a benefit concert. In the right setting and with proper amount of campus-wide support, a concert can be financially rewarding or, at least, bring good publicity to the library. Ideally, a successful benefit concert will become an annual event in which the library and its supporters can take pride each year. The music librarian must remember that this work will take a major commitment of staff time and should weigh such an undertaking carefully against other library goals and priorities.

FREE CONCERTS

An alternative to library fundraising concerts is to present free concerts. Such concerts eliminate the pressure to raise money while still promoting the library and educating people about its value to the college. Free concerts can nevertheless take a large amount of time and effort—but they are generally less work than concerts that charge admission. For example, free concerts occur at the MIT Lewis Music Library, where students and faculty perform occasionally in the library, often highlighting music from the library's collection. These are usually one-time concerts, although a concert highlighting a donation of violin music with student performers has become an annual event (see appendix 1, under "Violin Music Donation"). Some concerts are more adventurous than others. In 2005, MIT assistant music professor Brian Robison wrote a piece specifically for the music library entitled "Music in Stacks." In this work, audience members went into the music library stacks and chose music for Robison, who performed a few measures from each piece on his electric guitar. A sampler then "stacked" these phrases in real time as an improvised polyphony. Over fifty compositions were chosen by the audience, who delighted in this performance. The same professor also performed a Valentine's Day library concert entitled "Waves of Pleasure" in which he performed romantic music on the theremin. A standing-room-only audience filled the library for this concert. Unusual concert themes as well as high-profile performers will attract an audience. These free library concerts usually take place during a weekday at noon, with the objective of highlighting the library and its collections. The library justifies the time it puts into these concerts by judging many other intangibles, including the enthusiastic response that the concerts receive. Concerts showcase the library as a vibrant contributor to university life. Library concerts can serve many needs—just prepare to spend the time necessary in overseeing a myriad of details.

BOOK SALES

Another popular, if somewhat controversial, fundraiser for libraries is the book sale. On the surface, this appears to be a winning event for all parties involved. The library disposes of unwanted donations, library users and others purchase items at bargain prices, and the proceeds go to the library.

TESTING THE VALUE OF BOOK SALES

As with library concerts, however, book sales may require considerable staffing and entail certain hidden expenses. In order to test their profitability, Audrey Fenner, former head of the Acquisitions Department, Walter Clinton Jackson Library, University of North Carolina at Greensboro, conducted a cost-benefit analysis of three types of library book sales: annual sales, ongoing sales (that require no sales staff), and online sales. Detailed accounting considered the total staff time versus the amount of money raised, using the libraries at the University of North

Carolina at Greensboro and Missouri Western State College, St. Joseph, as models.[11] The conclusion from this study is clear-cut: library book sales are not profitable when considering staffing time. Fenner concludes:

> The models used here to analyze three methods of selling used books [annual sales, on-going sales, and online sales] indicate that there is a net financial loss rather than a net financial increase to the institution in each instance. These cost-benefit analyses indicate that book sales, whatever else they may be, are not effective fundraising activities. Systematic after-the-fact cost-benefit analyses are needed to determine if the methods of selling books that are described here can result in any actual profit or return for a library. How many book sales are conducted in libraries year after year just because it is assumed that they are profitable?[12]

Fenner also examined less traditional kinds of book sales, such as selling directly to book dealers, consignment sales through book dealers, book auctions, outsourcing the sales to groups outside of the library, and just giving the books away. In these cases, the costs were also too high and the monetary returns not enough to make them pay off from purely a financial viewpoint, although the author does acknowledge intangible public relation benefits.

Despite the negative conclusions reached in the Fenner study, other libraries feel that book sales are worth the effort. For instance, the University of Iowa assigned unwanted books to a book dealer on consignment. In this arrangement, the library was happy to collect 40 percent of the money raised while the dealer received 60 percent of the returns.[13] For those libraries with strong friends organizations, especially in public libraries, the traditional book sale still produces ample returns. Volunteers can help reduce staffing costs and allow libraries to make a profitable return. In Lancaster, Pennsylvania, the Lancaster Area Library Annual Book Sale raised $85,000 through a book sale held in a local skating rink, staffed by hundreds of volunteers.[14] Some libraries have found that they can increase their book sale profits by sorting out the most expensive titles and selling them separately to book dealers or collectors who are willing to pay more for rare and collectible items.

Online Booksellers

The future of library book sales may not involve the physical library space at all. Increasing numbers of libraries sell their unwanted materials through commercial booksellers' online websites.[15] Libraries pay a small commission for the privilege of selling their books online to a vast market. Some librarians recommend this method as a profitable way to raise money despite staffing costs. A pilot project at the University of Maryland's Engineering and Physical Sciences Library in 2003 sold unwanted books through Amazon.com and Half.com resulting in a net profit of $6,916.59.[16] The staff involved felt that this pilot raised more money with less staff time than the traditional book sale. The Friends of the Tucson-Pima Public Library in Arizona produced a revenue of almost $60,000 during fiscal year 2005–6 through internet sales on ABEbooks.com and Amazon.com.[17] In discussing this sale, Stephanie Gerding (continuing education coordinator at Arizona State Library, Archives and Public Records) and Mary Billings (general manager for the Friends of the Tucson-Pima Public Library) remarked, "With online book sales, you can place your inventory of discards and donations in front of millions of consumers and retailers, and sell at higher prices than would ordinarily be received at a regular book sale."[18] These libraries are not alone in their enthusiasm for online book sales. There are over five hundred libraries (mostly public) listed as members of an online book sale website, Library Book Sales (www.librarybooksales.org). An online bookseller that contributes to many social programs, Better World Books, also boasts large numbers, having "collected over 63 million books through active book drives at over 2,300 colleges and universities and collections from over 3,000 libraries."[19] There are many other online book sale vendors, and they will probably continue to attract libraries seeking to discard their unwanted materials.

ONLINE AUCTIONS

Online auctions are also popular with charitable organizations as a method of fundraising. The success of eBay and the public's familiarity with and attraction toward online auctions offer another venue for music libraries to consider.[20] As with online book sales, these auctions attract a national audience, therefore increasing the chances of more people bidding and higher sale prices. While some libraries use online auctions to acquire hard-to-locate or antiquarian books,[21] other libraries, especially public, sell their unwanted books through internet auctions.[22] It takes time, of course, for a library to set up an account and begin auctioning materials, although libraries' Friends groups, if available, might be able to handle much of the detail work. The library could limit its participation by offering just a few of the most expensive items. While online auctions can assist a library in selling unwanted materials to more people, the sense of community and bringing people into the physical library space is lost with online sales and auctions as well as the opportunity to personally meet new people and possibly identify potential new library supporters. Another side effect of online auctions in general is their appeal to potential thieves, who steal or check out expensive library books then auction them online for a price considerably higher than the library's fines and replacement costs.[23] Despite these drawbacks, online auctions will continue to attract public libraries and possibly more academic libraries as an effective means of selling unwanted books and other materials. As a variant to book selling, one public library even attempted to sell the naming rights to a new library building through eBay.[24] Music libraries may consider other creative methods of raising money through online auctions, especially if they target a list of potential bidders, such as interested alumni.

SELLING MUSIC MATERIALS

Music libraries have an advantage over other kinds of libraries in the types of materials that they offer at book sales. Because they receive donations in a variety of formats—including audio and video recordings, music scores, and music books—music library book sales appeal to a wide audience and can raise more money than general library book sales. The library should price most items to sell quickly but also be careful to charge for more attractive items accordingly. Because they are not in the business of selling used music materials, music librarians might want to consult the internet or even local vendors concerning any items that appear to be collectible. It is surprising how much money certain desirable books, scores, and record labels will command from those who know the used and antiquarian market. Rather than selling items themselves, some music libraries place their unwanted materials in a general library book sale with staff provided by other library personnel or friends organizations. This arrangement will reduce music library staffing time, but the proceeds from these sales may or may not be allocated to the music library.

Charities

The library could decide not to hold book sales at all but instead choose to give unwanted items away to charity. Doing so could cost the library some money in processing and shipping costs, but the satisfaction of helping others outweighs strictly monetary considerations. Donating unwanted materials will also send a message to library donors that your library not only takes in gifts but gives back as well. The International Association of Music Libraries, Archives and Documentation Centres plus the Music Library Association support a program in which music libraries can donate their unwanted books, scores, recordings, journals, and other items to those libraries in need. In the first ten years since its inception in 1995, the IAML-US Donated Music Materials Program initiated the donation of approximately 3,500 books and scores along with 400 periodical issues, and hundreds of recordings and videos.[25] The geographic scope of this program is widespread, including "libraries in East-Central and Southeast Europe, republics of the former Soviet Union, Africa, Asia, Latin America, and Pacific Ocean countries."[26] The MLA website includes a link to materials available from music libraries and individuals so that underprivileged libraries can check these inventories and request items that they want. The donating library is responsible for shipping costs, although libraries may apply for a Neil Ratliff IAML Outreach Grant to request reimbursement.[27] The American Library Association also provides advice on donating books and other materials to various book donation programs.[28] Other giving opportunities also arise periodically in response to disasters as they occur throughout the world. To assist in these calamities, postings on MLA-L (the Music Library Association's e-mail distribution list) invite music libraries to contribute their materials to those institutions in need of music. Libraries should consider these worthy options as a viable alternative to holding book sales.

Legal Restrictions

A few music libraries choose not to hold book sales due to legal issues and interpretations of IRS laws. Some state universities do not allow libraries to sell donated materials because they consider these items to be "state property" which is not to be sold under state law. There may also be concern about selling materials for which donors have already taken a tax deduction, as well as the interpretation that libraries should not sell any materials due to their institutions' tax-exempt status. Because of possible legal concerns, librarians should seek official library and university approval before initiating any kind of music library book sales.

Raising funds through library book sales, whether in-house or online, can be fun and exhilarating, especially for librarians who are not in the business of collecting money other than a few annoying overdue fines at the circulation desk. Bringing in cash at sales provides a certain feeling of accomplishment. Libraries should be wary, however, of falling prey to the enticement of book sales and the prospect of making large amounts of money. Would music libraries be wise to simply eliminate book sales? Not necessarily. Libraries need to consider their own set of circumstances. The library should assess the success and economics of conducting book sales in relation to broader library priorities. As mentioned previously, one very real benefit of book sales held in libraries is the publicity and goodwill that they generate. Of course, this aspect is less tangible and more difficult to assess. New users and friends sometimes discover the library through book sales. Students may be eternally grateful to the library for providing them with that Eulenberg miniature score of a Beethoven symphony for twenty-five cents. The library may establish lasting relationships with donors through these events, proving that the real value of library book sales does not necessarily lie with the bottom line. If a library feels that such publicity is rich in building relationships, it might want to continue holding book sales even though they may not be profitable strictly from a cost-benefit perspective.

OTHER PUBLIC EVENTS

Music libraries can offer other types of events, both in the library and elsewhere, such as lectures, lecture/recitals, and panel discussions. Well-known music faculty members or prominent guest speakers will attract a certain following and produce sizable audiences. The library can often connect its holdings to the subject of the event by highlighting library materials on display or through bibliographies that may inspire people to explore the library further. If the library has a mailing list, it can collect new names at events to build up the library's donor database. The library can charge for admission or events can be free. Events may cost the library money, but the long-term payoffs could be worth the time and effort. Try to invite local donors to attend library events in order to show them the vitality of your library and the ways in which it connects to the community at your institution. If a donor who helped to sponsor an event is present, be sure to acknowledge that person publically. Public acknowledgement of donors at events underscores the library's appreciation of their support and makes donors feel a connection to the library. But also be aware of the inherent danger of public acknowledgements. If you announce specific names, you may inadvertently omit another donor who is present. Leaving out just one name can cause hurt feelings for a donor and embarrassment for the library.

For nonacademic events, public libraries concoct some of the most inventive and original fundraising ideas. One especially imaginative example, although not a musical one, was a Cow

Pie Bingo held by the Friends of the Adamstown Area (PA) Library. In this event, a ball field served as a giant bingo card with lines drawn and two hundred numbers arranged within the squares. People placed their bets by paying $10 per square. Three cows then wandered around the field until the first "cow pie" dropped into one of the boxes. All two hundred boxes were sold, the winner received $500, and the library collected the remaining money.[29] It is fun to imagine this event on our central campus greens, but even the most adventurous university development staff would probably consider this proposal to be beyond the bounds of academic sanity. With their strong emphasis on community outreach and multitude of volunteers, public libraries sometimes sponsor events not otherwise feasible in academic settings.

Friends of the Library groups often have creative ideas for library events while they also provide the staffing to carry them out. Music librarian Marian Ritter at Western Washington University established a remarkable Friends of the Music Library group in 1996 that helps to organize and run book sales, library receptions, and dinners. This group sponsors chartered bus trips to the Seattle Symphony and Vancouver Opera and has assisted in organizing group cruises to Alaska as well as jazz galas and chamber music concerts. The friends assist in preparing the music library's newsletter, and they even write letters and acknowledgements to the membership. A key to the success of this friends organization is a core of dedicated and hard-working board members who help to organize these activities. By 2005, these energetic friends helped to raise approximately $40,000 to purchase editions of composers' collected works for the library.[30] Another friends group worth noting is the Carnegie Library of Pittsburgh's Friends of the Music Library (FML), which was established in 1938. This venerable organization holds an annual fundraising letter campaign in addition to successful book sales that support the music collection. According to the Carnegie Library of Pittsburgh website, ". . . the healthy growth of the collection has been due in great part to the generous annual gifts from the FML."[31]

These success stories, however, are not necessarily the norm. Some academic libraries avoid friends groups altogether because of the time and effort that they can create for a library staff. Working with friends groups does not always justify the end results. According to Kimberly A. Thompson (director of library development and outreach at the University of California, Santa Barbara) and Karlene Noel Jennings (director of library development for the Earl Gregg Swem Library at the College of William and Mary), "Friends groups continue to be great sources of support for public libraries, but the ever-changing academic landscape appears to be altering their ability to play a meaningful role."[32] As libraries reduce staffs and streamline operations, they will closely scrutinize friends groups and the actual payoff that they provide.[33]

PRIVATE EVENTS FOR MAJOR DONORS

In addition to events open to the general library community, library development also calls for sophisticated private events that focus on thanking and honoring major donors who contribute significantly to the library. These invitation-only events often occur in elaborate and costly settings especially if the university has a healthy development office. The reasons for such events will vary. The library may honor a donor for a recent contribution. There could also be celebrations, such as the anniversary of a renovation or the opening of new building, that recognize major library donors for their support. The centerpiece of these events is often a lunch, dinner, reception, lecture, or some other gathering. The music library is unlikely to have the financial resources or expertise to sponsor such affairs. The development office usually pays the expenses and orchestrates the details, including the choice of printed invitations/menus/programs, food, beverages, china, crystal, silverware, table cloths, napkins, flowers, photographer, musicians, and so on. The development office will carefully choose the speakers who will eloquently thank the donors. The professional caterers and event planners will not overlook any detail of such well-choreographed events. The expenses for such occasions may seem excessive, especially in an academic setting. The music library staff members can only imagine all the books and scores that they could purchase with that money. But the development staff will confidently justify these expenses by reiterating their oft-repeated adage, "It takes money to make money." Development professionals also recognize the fact that those people who have already donated money are prime candidates to contribute again. Individuals invited to these gatherings are usually not solicited at the events. Instead, development staff will later find ways through mailings or personal contacts to suggest that contributions would be welcome. Of course, if the donor has just contributed a multi-million dollar gift, the development staff will probably wait a respectful period before asking for more.

Chapter Five

CORPORATIONS, FOUNDATIONS, AND GOVERNMENT GRANTS

OVERVIEW

The world of corporate, foundation, and government grants may seem far removed from the small-scale fundraising activity generally engaged in by your average music library. These types of grants merit attention, however, for two important reasons. First, these organizations offer a substantial number of grants targeted specifically for music library projects. Second, the size of the grants available from these organizations can often be considerable. In recent years, foundations and government agencies have demonstrated particular interest in funding projects that preserve and make accessible unique and rare materials that will enrich our national culture. Preservation and digitization of unique or unusual music materials are highly fundable projects which can benefit musicians and scholars around the world. Foundations and government agencies are most likely to award significant amounts of money to music library projects that will benefit the broadest range of library patrons; private institutions can usually qualify for funding of such projects if they agree in turn to permit access to the musical materials treated in the project. Corporations, on the other hand, are more likely to support smaller projects that fall within their immediate geographic areas. Their grant awards often benefit only the specific needs of a particular library and its patrons, but they are still viewed by the corporation as a meaningful way to give back to the community.

INSTITUTIONAL APPROVAL

As with all the other fundraising initiatives discussed in this book, the music librarian must communicate from the outset with the development office about any potential proposal for corporate, foundation, or government grants. Since these organizations are a major source of outside funding for most institutions, the librarian has to be especially careful to identify music library projects in which these organizations have demonstrated special interest. The music library should never compete with any initiative which the development office may plan to submit to an organization.

Before commencing any grant application to a corporation, foundation, or government agency, the music librarian should seek formal approval from the development office. Such projects almost always impose some strain on an institution's resources; senior administrators need to weigh the overall costs of administering a project versus the benefit to the institution as a whole, not just the benefit to the music library. Potential costs to the institution include the management and dispersal of the grant money, which will be handled and tracked by the institution's business office; the staff time required to write and administer a grant; the staff time needed to carry out the grant activities; and possibly the space and materials needed to support it. Government grants, in particular, usually require the institution to commit some percentage of matching support in an application. And, many universities charge overhead, a percentage of the total project budget, which is expected to be included in the total requested under the grant. Some funders do not subsidize overhead, so the applicant must lobby for a deferral of overhead from the university or find the money elsewhere. At some institutions the overhead can be over half of the total project budget, so finding the money within the library budget can be challenging and time consuming, as can be the process of requesting a waiver.

Because the development of a music library grant project will require specialized knowledge and experience, the music librarian should offer to assist with every facet of its implementation–establishing the project goals, timeline and activities, developing the budget, and identifying the staff and material requirements. If at all possible, the librarian should offer to assist with writing the application, administering the project, and providing any reports that may be required. The music librarian's ability and willingness to assist with these time-consuming responsibilities can help to relieve the burden on the development staff and could go a long way to obtaining the necessary institutional approval. The process of writing grants can be long and involved. There are a number of publications that provide advice on how to write a successful grant proposal and how to implement grant funding once it is obtained.[1]

The music librarian should carefully consider the pros and cons of developing any major grant project. The prospect of receiving a major, one-time award is enticing, if only for the recognition it bestows on the music library. On the other hand, awards from a corporation, foundation or government agency require more effort in return than simply writing a thank-you note. The music librarian must decide whether the value of the project is worth the amount of time required to achieve the project goals. Government grants, in particular, can be especially time consuming; they always involve long, detailed applications, thorough reporting, and rigorous evidence of project results.

CORPORATIONS

Your institution's development office has most likely plumbed the mine of corporate funding possibilities within the geographic area surrounding your institution. Corporations, for the most part, seek to support local institutions and projects that benefit their particular community. Keep in mind the interests of the corporation and try to form a partnership in which both the library and corporation will benefit. In addition to grant money, corporations will often supply in-kind gifts, services, use of their facilities, and even volunteers from their workforce.

The easiest way for the music librarian to avoid competing with the institution's corporate ties is to identify specific materials or projects that could benefit the library. Does the library need to upgrade its audio equipment, replace worn furniture, or acquire additional computing or scanning equipment? Such gifts can provide considerable relief to the library budget and, in the long term, require relatively little effort from the librarian. Are there any volunteer partnerships from a corporation that might benefit the library? While working with volunteers can take a great deal of staff time, the right match could bring a new level of expertise and experience in a much needed area. The best means of identifying a potential corporate sponsor for the music library is to contact staff members in the development office who deal specifically with corporate partnerships and contributions. This staff can usually assist in making the contact with the appropriate corporation and arranging for the donation. Sometimes the contact will be made by one of the institution's board members to a friend on the board or senior management of a corporation who might have an interest in the music library and its needs.

The music librarian should take care, however, to clearly describe the library's minimum requirements for a corporate gift in kind. The library is not a junkyard for equipment that the corporation has not been able to unload. On the contrary, the music library can be a showcase for quality furniture and equipment. The corporation, in turn, should be allowed to market the fact that the John Smith Music Library in Centerville is proud to provide its students and faculty with their headphones, high-speed scanners, and so on. The library can reciprocate additionally by offering to display a corporation's name or logo, with approval from library and university leadership.

If your development office does not have information on corporations, helpful resources include the Foundation Center's *National Directory of Corporate Giving* (print edition) and *Corporate Giving Online*. The latter title supplies detailed online information covering 3,800 company profiles and records of over 380,000 recently awarded grants. Many corporations provide matching gifts for their employees' charitable contributions. Corporations' monetary funding through grants is often dependent upon a company's profits from year to year. To make their charitable donations more consistent, corporations establish foundations with endowed money so that they can distribute grant money over the long term.

FOUNDATIONS

Grantmaking foundations are nonprofit organizations that support their philanthropic missions by funding educational, social, health-related, cultural, or other charitable causes. Of all grant-issuing establishments, foundations are probably the most misunderstood. Studies have found that approximately 80 percent of all applications to private foundations are inappropriate and not eligible for funding.[2] Private foundations provide a major source of funding to not-for-profit institutions since they are required to give away a minimum amount of money annually in order to retain their tax status under Section 501(c)(3) of the Internal Revenue Code. Funding from foundations varies in size from hundreds to millions of dollars per grant. Foundations are overseen by governing boards to manage their programs and make their grantmaking decisions. Larger foundations will have a professional staff to handle processing of applications and day-to-day operations, but decisions on who receives money are generally made by the trustees. These tax-exempt organizations report their annual giving figures through the Internal Revenue Service's Form 990-PF which is publically available, free of charge, at the GuideStar website: www.guidestar.org.[3]

Types of Foundations

According to *The Foundation Directory*, the major types of private and community grant-making foundations encompass four categories: independent foundations, company-sponsored foundations, operating foundations, and community foundations.[4]

Independent foundations are also known sometimes as "family foundations" because members of philanthropic families often establish and direct them. These private foundations support grant proposals both narrow and broad as long as they enhance the vision established by their founders. Independent foundations fund projects located within a close geographic proximity to their headquarters in about 70 percent of the grants they award.[5]

Company-sponsored foundations fund projects that reflect a corporation's focus and interests. Although supported by their parent companies, company-sponsored foundations are separate legal entities. These private foundations often favor grant requests for projects in geographic locations near their corporate operations.

Operating foundations furnish grants to help run their own organizations' services, research, or programs. Income for these foundations is commonly provided through a single endowment, but they also accept donations from the public. This type of private foundation sometimes awards a limited number of grants for specific purposes, but they are typically an unlikely source of grant funding for music libraries. Examples of operating foundations include museums, zoos, and performing arts spaces.

Community foundations provide a variety of grants to charitable organizations within the local vicinity of the foundations. These publically sponsored foundations count on donations from multiple sources, unlike private foundations, which ordinarily rely upon single-source funding. The IRS usually considers community foundations to be public charities. Typically, grant-funding decisions are made by a board of directors with close ties to a particular region or community.[6] A board bases its decisions on a clearly defined set of goals or programs related to the local community. Community foundations often manage donor advised funds as well. In this instance, donors are able to direct how to disburse the income from their specific fund. Generally, grants from donor advised funds are raised as individual gifts from these donors and do not require formal grant proposals.

The Andrew W. Mellon Foundation

One of the best known independent foundations that has generously supported library projects over the years is the Andrew W. Mellon Foundation. Both JSTOR and ARTstor received their initial funding from Mellon before they became financially independent nonprofit organizations. In 2010, Mellon's Libraries and Scholarly Communications Program merged with the Research in Information Technology Program to form the Scholarly Communications and Information Technology Program, one of its five core program areas. The scope of this program, as described on the Mellon website, includes several areas that relate to libraries:

> Scholarly communications covers a broad range of activities, including the discovery, collection, organization, evaluation, interpretation, and preservation of primary and other sources of information, and the publication and dissemination of scholarly research. . . . Information technology includes the design, development, implementation, and support of computer-based systems for converting, storing, protecting, processing, retrieving, and transmitting information in electronic form.[7]

Although most music librarians may only be familiar with the larger-scale music library projects funded by Mellon, the foundation has a long record of support for institutions of all sizes. In 2010, Mellon's annual report listed awards totaling $29,855,500 given through its Scholarly Communications and Information Technology Program. Institutions received ninety-four grants that year, ranging in size from $7,500 to $1,293,000.[8] Some of this funding was awarded to music projects at universities or performing institutions with library materials.

Given the substantial amount of money it awards to libraries of all types on an annual basis, Mellon is certainly a major source to be considered for any project that falls within the goals of its funding program. As with any foundation that supports a broad range of projects in higher education and in the arts, the music library's parent institution may have other proposals in mind for Mellon support that would take precedence over one from the library. Discuss any potential proposal to Mellon at the outset with your development office.

PURSUING FOUNDATION GRANT FUNDING

With thousands of other foundations giving billions of dollars each year, how do libraries find the right grant funding for their projects? A music library may have a proposal that would match the giving parameters of a particular foundation, but the librarian may not have time to research and locate that one resource. Rather than give up, the librarian should check initially with appropriate staff within the library system to see if a foundation grant would be worth pursuing. To begin the process, it helps to write a short, concise project outline with a realistic budget and a summary of the grant's benefits. Keep in mind that researching and writing a grant proposal takes considerable effort, and that a successful proposal would mean even more work for the library in carrying out the project. Librarians must weigh the possible benefits in relation to other library priorities. They should also have realistic expectations. Weeks and months of grant application work might result in successful funding that significantly improves the library, or it could result in no funding at all.

With library approval, the grant proposal can go forward to the development office. The proposal should be clear, concise, and easily understood by a nonlibrarian. The development staff will likely have knowledge of specific foundations that are appropriate for the project. They will look for a match between the library project and the scope of foundations' giving parameters, such as geographic location, size of awards, and specific subject areas. The development staff may suggest that the library fine tune parts of the topic in order to better match a foundation's requirements. The university's overall pursuit of grants must be considered as well. One foundation might appear to be the ideal funding source for a music library project, but the development office may have another department's proposal in mind for that same foundation grant. As with all development work, the music librarian must cooperate with the development office and understand the bigger fundraising picture of the university.

Foundation Directories and Other Resources

Not all music librarians have the luxury of a development office's expertise to guide them towards a foundation grant. They may need to conduct some or all of the research on their own. A good starting point is the nonprofit Foundation Center, which issues a variety of print and online sources concerning foundations. *The Foundation Directory* is probably the best-known resource for finding information on nongovernment, nonprofit foundations. This extensive annual print volume includes information on the nation's ten thousand largest giving organizations. A companion volume entitled *The Foundation Directory Part 2* lists the next largest ten thousand foundations. Searching is facilitated by seven indexes arranged by names of donors, officers, trustees; geographic locations; international giving interests; types of support; subject areas; foundations new to the current edition; and foundation names. Descriptive entries of foundations' funding are listed by U.S. states and territories with thirty-four data elements given for each organization. Particularly helpful is information about recent grant recipients, which includes short descriptions of winning proposals along with the amount of funding granted. Detailed indexing in Foundation Center publications makes it easy to locate specific information quickly.

The Foundation Directory Online is also available with various subscription plans that range in coverage from ten thousand to one hundred thousand U.S. foundations, corporate donors, and grant-making public charities. The Foundation Center's *Grants for Libraries & Information Services, 2011 Digital Edition*, issued as a downloadable PDF file, includes descriptions of nearly 2,700 grants that total over $565 million from 701 foundations. Also produced by the Foundation Center is *Grants for Arts, Culture, & the Humanities, 2011 Digital Edition*, a downloadable PDF file that describes over 24,700 grants worth nearly $3 billion from 1,195 foundations. If your library and development office lack these Foundation Center materials, there are Foundation Center Cooperating Collections located throughout the country in libraries and other facilities that provide Foundation Center online and print publications to the public at no cost.[9] It is also possible to register on the Foundation Center mailing list and obtain free information, including monthly online newsletters covering different subjects—for example, "Arts Funding Watch" and "Education Funding Watch."

The Directory of Music Foundations, 2009–2010 covers foundations from around the world, including approximately ninety U.S. foundations that provide grants supporting music projects. Music fundraisers with an international perspective might find this book to be useful. This print publication (also available on CD-ROM) includes limited subject indexing, however, and little detail concerning each foundation, making it unclear whether libraries are eligible for funding. To obtain a greater level of detail, it helps to supplement this book with other resources, such as the Foundation Center publications or a specific foundation's own website.

Besides foundation guides, there are resources that cover a broad range of funding sources for library grants. A print newsletter that focuses on library grants is *Grants for Libraries Hotline*, which appears in twelve monthly issues with weekly e-mail updates. The subscription cost includes an annual index. This newsletter lists types of grants arranged by subject, amount of money available, deadlines, and contact information. In addition to this publication, there are valuable sources of grant information available at no cost. The *Library Grants* blog (http://librarygrants.blogspot.com), written by Stephanie K. Gerding and Pamela H. MacKellar, presents grant opportunities for libraries. GrantsAlert.com (http://www.grantsalert.com/about.cfm) is a website that focuses on grants for school libraries. Although both of these resources are geared toward nonacademic libraries, they include grants of interest to academic libraries as well. The Foundation Center's *Philanthropy News Digest (PND)* (http://foundationcenter.org/pnd/) provides daily grant news updates and lists new grants offered by grant-making organizations and nonprofits with application details available in requests for proposals or RFPs. These are just a few of the resources available on the internet. As Nancy K. Herther, sociology/anthropology librarian at the University of Minnesota, points out, "Virtually all foundations now have well-designed web pages, as do associations and other key organizations. With a little creative brainstorming and careful searching, you may find that you don't need to go further than your own computer to get information to secure the funding that you or your client needs."[10]

GRANT PAYMENT OPTIONS

In considering foundation grants, it helps to know some of the variant grant payment options that may be available. While grants usually consist of an organization providing a lump sum of money to an applicant, there are other methods of payment. A matching grant allows two or more organizations to share the cost of a grant. Such a match usually involves a grant proposal in which the applicant must find another source of funding that will equal the initial requested amount. This type of matching grant is called a 1:1 match. For example, a foundation may match the amount that a library will provide or raise from other donors as part of the grant. Sometimes a challenge grant is suggested by a grant-making entity, in which the grant is used as incentive to raise funds from a number of other donors to support the project. Individuals have also been known to sponsor challenge grants. Seed grants provide funding to begin a new project or conduct a thorough business plan for an extensive project, with the expectation that this project will later obtain larger amounts of support to expand and complete the work. This kind of funding is also known as start-up money.

GOVERNMENT GRANTS

THE INSTITUTE OF MUSEUM AND LIBRARY SERVICES

The major government funding agency for museums and libraries of all types is the Institute of Museum and Library Services (IMLS). Although a federal agency, it works in coordination with state and local organizations to "sustain heritage, culture, and knowledge; enhance learning and innovation; and support professional development."[11] The Museum and Library Services Act authorizes the institute to support two major activities: the Library Services and Technology Act (LSTA) and the Museum Services Act (MSA).

Through LSTA, millions of dollars are distributed annually to state library agencies across the country. These agencies develop long-range plans that establish library service priorities for their state; they are responsible for conducting LSTA grant rounds and making the awards. Depending on the scope of the project, LSTA awards can range from a few thousand dollars to hundreds of thousands of dollars. In general, they tend to fund projects in the areas of resource sharing, user education, technology innovation and expansion, community outreach, and preservation of cultural heritage. Although funding priorities will vary from state to state, a quick search of the Internet reveals that numerous music library projects have been funded with LSTA money during the past few years.

The IMLS website lists nineteen named grant awards, of which seven are designated as appropriate for library institutions. Of these awards, the National Leadership Grants, in particular, has funded several music library projects or projects that involved music materials. Unlike the LSTA awards, which are administered through the state, the IMLS named grants are awarded directly by the IMLS; its website provides complete descriptions of each grant award, including funding priorities, eligibility requirements and lists of previous recipients.

NARA, NHPRC, AND NEH

Although the IMLS is the only government agency whose sole mission is to support museums and libraries, there are twenty-five additional federal grant-funding agencies, some of which have provided substantial awards to music library projects. Of these, the most important agencies for music libraries over the past several years have been the National Archives and Records Administration (NARA), and the National Endowment for the Humanities (NEH). Some of the largest projects funded by them have been undertaken by major universities; many of these are well known in the music library profession and have made significant contributions to our musical culture. These agencies have also funded smaller institutions as well, however, and should be considered when contemplating any project that involves important and unique material, regardless of the size of the collection.

The grant-making affiliate of NARA is the National Historical Publications and Records Commission (NHPRC). Each year, Congress appropriates up to $10 million for NHPRC grants, including projects to edit and publish historical records of national importance, to research and develop means to preserve authentic electronic records, and to preserve and make accessible records and archives. This funding source, in particular, has benefited many smaller institutions and libraries that care for unique and historically valuable collections but have lacked the resources to begin a formal program to organize and make them accessible. Over the years, the NHPRC has enabled a number of smaller music schools to establish comprehensive archives and records management programs in their libraries, benefitting not only the institution and its immediate community but helping to preserve and make accessible historical materials of value to our national musical heritage. The NHPRC has also funded preservation and access projects for several unique music collections of national historical significance.

The NEH is another major source of grant funding for museums, archives, libraries, colleges, universities, public television, and radio stations. Dedicated to supporting research, education, preservation, and public programs in the humanities, the NEH is divided into nine divisions, each of which has its own separate programs. A website search of funded programs indicates libraries are funded with grants that vary in size from approximately $2,000 to $500,000.[12] Most of these grants were awarded through the Office of Digital Humanities, the Division of Preservation and Access, the Division of Public Programs, and the Division of Research Programs. Recipients range from large universities to small private institutions. Some of the most recent awards have funded large-scale digitization projects of music materials, not only insuring their preservation but making them immediately accessible over the web.

Pursuing Government Grant Funding

While the IMLS, NHRPC and NEH all have a long history of generous support for music library projects, a distinct advantage for the academic music library in applying for IMLS funds is the agency's exclusive mission to support museums and libraries. Any IMLS grant application from the library will not be in competition with other projects outside the library at your university. The NEH, however, could be an important source of grant money for other educational projects at the institution. If so, the library may have difficulty convincing the administration to put forward the music library project for NEH funding. As mentioned above, the librarian should always consult first with the institution's development office before developing plans for any grant application to a government agency.

One of the most serious considerations before embarking on a government grant application is the considerable amount of time required to prepare it. One person could easily spend as much as sixty to seventy hours gathering institutional data, preparing the project budget, developing a project work-plan and time-line, as well as writing a comprehensive project narrative. This is basic information required for any government application, regardless of the funding agency. Depending on the competition with similar projects from around the country, the odds of receiving an award could be low. The music librarian will need to assure the parent institution that there is a chance of success with the proposed application.

The best measuring stick for success with a government grant application is the fact that a library similar in size and function to yours has already received an award for the type of project you want to fund. Since each agency keeps an updated list of grant awards on its website, this type of information is readily available over the internet. Often, success stories from music librarian colleagues will inspire the idea to develop a grant project.

Grant agencies are most concerned that the projects they fund will achieve their stated goals. They look closely to determine that the grant requestor is an established institution able to contribute its matching share of the budget, that the project staff has the necessary qualifications to accomplish the work of the project, and that the project work-plan and timeline is adequate for the established goals. If the application meets all of these criteria, the application has a stronger chance of receiving funding. Above all, the funding agency needs to recognize the significance of the project. An ideal project involves music materials that are important to the nation's musical culture and will become easily accessible through the internet as a result of the project. Projects that include music materials still under copyright protection and subject to restricted access over the internet, or not accessible at all outside the institution, are less likely to be funded than projects that are able to make materials readily available to the public. Projects that can also serve as models for other libraries have an even greater chance of obtaining an award.

If the music librarian feels confident that the project has significance and that institutional support is in place to achieve the project goals, the effort required to pull together a government grant application is probably worth putting forth. Above all, the library receives the financial resources to accomplish what it may never be able to do alone, or at least not for the foreseeable future. A government grant award also brings distinction to the library and the parent institution as well as positive publicity at the national level. Successful completion of a government-funded project also strengthens the music library's ability to succeed with future grant applications to another funding agency.

The Application Process

The grant cycle for government awards can span the better part of a year, from the date of the application deadline to the date of the actual award announcement and the date that funds are actually issued. Start dates vary from agency to agency and program to program. Projects themselves typically span one to three years. Occasionally, large-scale projects are eligible to apply for renewal of one to three years, depending on availability of funds. Grant applications to any government agency are only accepted electronically, at the website http://grants.gov. Each institution must register at this website before any application can be submitted. Grant application packets, however, may be downloaded without registering at the grants website. In addition to the required institutional data, each granting agency will require some or several attachments in support of the application.

Key to each application is a detailed budget sufficient to achieve the goals of the project. In developing the budget, the institution is required to share in the actual cost of the project.

This contribution can often be calculated in terms of contributed staff time, not only the direct salary paid by the institution but employee benefits paid as well. The government also allows a certain percentage for overhead to count towards the institution's contribution. Most often, the largest project expense is designated for staff salaries, but money for equipment, supplies, and so forth can be requested as well. Projects extending beyond one year should include a salary raise for each additional year for all staff members listed in the budget. The total budget request should not exceed the award ranges established for the award category; on the other hand, there is no reward for underestimating the costs for project activities. The granting agency will not look favorably on a budget that does not realistically support the project.

The project narrative is the core of the application. In the narrative, the applicant should write convincingly about the worth and soundness of the project. The narrative plan must state clearly achievable goals and the methods that will be used to assess whether these goals are achieved. The narrative should also discuss the qualifications of the principal investigator (the person designated to head the proposed project; abbreviated "PI") and of the staff and any experience that the institution has relative to the planned activities in the project. Supporting documents requested will generally include curriculum vitae for all staff involved in the project.

Letters of support also give evidence of the feasibility and significance of your project. The application will often request letters of commitment from the senior administration in the institution, preferably the president or director, and also letters of support from recognized professionals who can speak with authority on the value and credibility of your project proposal. Ideally, you should solicit support from senior members in the music library profession who would value the goals of the project. Their input could have a significant influence on the granting agency's decision.

Although the government-grant writing process may seem fairly daunting to the novice fundraiser, government agencies themselves are committed to helping applicants submit strong proposals. Agency staff members are available to answer questions and offer advice whenever needed. They are probably your best resource when trying to assess whether your project meets the funding objectives of the agency. Often, the agency will provide the opportunity during the grant application cycle to submit a draft for formal comment. Issues with the project budget, work plan and activities, and so on can be raised and addressed at this time, thus strengthening the application and its chances for an award. It is advisable, however, to get clearance from your development officer prior to contacting a program officer from any grant-making agency or foundation.

Administering Government Grant Projects

Once a grant is awarded and the project begins, the PI keeps careful track of the project activities and a close eye on the project timeline. During the grant-funded phase of the project, the PI will be required to submit regular reports on the progress of the project and on the expenditure of the project funds. Any change in the project plan or timeline will be mentioned in these reports. At the completion of the grant-funded phase, the project director must submit a complete report on the project and the distribution of funds, according to the guidelines of the funding agency. Any products that were promised as a result of the project must be delivered at the time specified in the application.

The effort and time involved in administrating a government-funded project can seem overwhelming. The grant-making agencies require thorough planning, attention to detail and steady progress toward the project goals. In the long run, however, government grant guidelines and regulations provide an excellent structure for a grant-funded project and help to ensure that the library will succeed in meeting its project goals.

OTHER GRANT OPPORTUNITIES

Corporate, foundation, and government grants may offer the best possibilities for funding large and expensive music library projects, but there are also options for grants on a less generous scale. Many of these smaller-sized grants might be available in the library's own campus and certainly require much less effort to obtain. Here are a few local grant possibilities to consider.

University Resources

Some universities provide grant information on their development office websites, which include features such as searchable databases, details on upcoming grants, and print/online resources.[13] Universities may also offer funding for small grants that are available only to departments or organizations within the campus. One such example is the Council for the Arts at MIT, which was established in 1972 to support MIT's visual, literary, and performing arts. Since 1974, the council's grants program has provided over $2.5 million in grant money to support over 2,500 arts projects created by the MIT community.[14] The Lewis Music Library receives various grants through this program, ranging from library materials that support new music courses to funding for library concerts and lectures. Since these grants are awarded three times a year, there is little waiting time between the application deadline and the award announcements. Grant amounts are relatively small, ranging in size from $500 to a few thousand dollars, but these awards can come in handy for covering expenses that the library could not afford otherwise. Do not overlook such grants on campus that could be readily available.

Professional Societies and Associations

Small grants are available through professional societies and associations. The Music Library Association offers grants not to libraries but to individual librarians in support of travel, conducting research, or attending MLA meetings ("Awards and Grants," http://musiclibraryassoc.org/awards.aspx?id=42). Librarians involved with other library associations may find similar grants available to society members. In particular, the American Library Association awards a number of small grants encompassing a wide spectrum of topics that include staff development, research assistance, collection development, and many more ("Awards & Grants," http://www.ala.org/ala/awardsgrants/index.cfm). The Association for Recorded Sound Collections offers grants, ranging in size from $2,000 to $10,000, to music libraries and other music organizations for projects "to encourage and support the preservation of historically significant sound recordings of Western Art Music by individuals and organizations."[15]

COMMUNITY AND LOCAL ORGANIZATIONS

Local businesses and organizations sometimes award relatively small amounts of money or gifts in kind to individuals and establishments within their communities. Universities and academic music libraries may want to investigate whether they are eligible for this funding. Although the librarian may have personal contacts with local businesses or organizations, remember that these establishments often have limited resources to donate. Judge the potential giving power of an organization before pursuing a gift. The local bakery may be willing to donate some delicious brownies to a benefit concert, but it is unlikely that the baker would be able to fund the renovation of a library. As with other grant resources, always check with a development officer before pursuing any grant applications.

Chapter Six

ISSUES TO CONSIDER IN FUNDRAISING

HIDDEN COSTS

While fundraising for the music library has enormous benefits, the library staff should consider certain hidden costs before it begins to raise money. In the discussions thus far, a recurring theme is that fundraising requires considerable staff time. Fundraising events and writing grants may seem simple enough to accomplish but they can take much more time than anticipated. Similarly, the entire cycle of identifying, cultivating, soliciting, and stewarding donors represents many hours of effort. Unless a music library has the unlikely advantage of a development staff doing all of its fundraising work, the music librarian will need to decide how to accomplish these new responsibilities with a staff that may already be overworked.

Another issue is the subtle way in which fundraising work can expand over time, gaining a momentum and life of its own. Development work can imperceptibly alter the nature of jobs. With successful fundraising, the number of donors will grow steadily, thus adding responsibilities and demands upon a library staff that may not realize the extent to which these activities have increased until some aspects of workers' jobs begin to suffer. The music library should examine its priorities periodically to see if fundraising, with its positives and negatives, is providing an overall benefit to the library. Is fundraising worth the effort if the library has to give up certain activities or services? In the end, job descriptions may need adjustment in order to accommodate new fundraising endeavors. Openly examine these changes before adding a few fundraising activities to the workload with the hope that the staff will manage successfully over time. Keep a written list of realistic goals and objectives for the long and short term to review regularly. Seek advice from the library or institutional development staff and see if they will assist with any fundraising responsibilities.

If a music library raises funds for a one-time project such as a renovation, its staff could spend months, even years, in the planning and implementation of this work. While this requires intense work, the project has a finite timeline. On the other hand, obtaining donations, both monetary and gifts in kind, to support the collection can be an ongoing activity that impacts a wide number of staff members throughout an entire library system. Libraries operate with an annual budget that covers certain projected costs during a year. Fundraising can throw these anticipated expenses off balance due to the added costs associated with an influx of new materials. Consider a hypothetical case in which a music library raises $3,000 to purchase collection materials. The music librarian is ecstatic to think of the all the new books, scores, and recordings that this money can purchase. The library publicizes its success throughout the campus and to its donors. In mentioning this triumph to library colleagues in acquisitions, cataloging, and processing, however, the librarian detects a less than enthusiastic response. The librarian soon realizes that the library's regular budget was not set up to process, catalog, and store that many additional new materials in a single year. The music library may be able to purchase these items but they will not be available to users for an indefinite time period. The librarian also finds that selecting more materials to order with this extra money takes several hours from an already busy schedule. Now imagine the same scenario but with donations that equal $30,000 rather than $3,000. How would the library staff be able to absorb this amount of work into its normal work load? Raising money can be relatively easy when compared to the other library work required to make new materials ready for circulation. Many of these staffing issues also apply to gifts in kind. As mentioned previously, materials donated to the library are not really free. They come with a cost. It was estimated in 2005 that each donated item added to a library actually cost approximately $45 in staffing and processing expenses.[1] Such "free" materials can become a rather substantial investment.

Before implementing any fundraising effort, the music library should talk to various departments within the library that could be affected by an onslaught of new materials. Ask about staffing provisions that might be available in case fundraising initiatives are successful. Are there limits to the number of gifts in kind and purchased items that the library processes, catalogs, and shelves? Can the library provide additional staff members to cover these costs? If new help is not possible and the music library cannot rearrange job assignments to accomplish this work, the staff will need to re-examine its fundraising goals. It is essential to continually scrutinize the consequences of fundraising and its impact upon a staff's time.

Here is another scenario that touches upon staffing. In this case, a music librarian raises $25,000 in the first two years of fundraising. On the surface, this appears to be a highly successful effort, but there could be hidden costs if we consider the librarian's work that suffered due to fundraising. This librarian may not even be aware of spending less time at the music library reference desk where student assistants now fill in. The librarian also reduced the number of lunches and informal meetings previously enjoyed with music faculty and fellow librarians. Visiting with donor prospects made the librarian less available within the library as well. Perhaps the librarian also took shortcuts in collection development work, deciding not to read as many reviews as before. Is the donated money worth the librarian sacrificing job responsibilities? What, on the other hand, if the same librarian had raised $5 million for the library? Would that amount of money be worth the librarian's time? These are questions to consider and judge within the context of each individual music library. Remember, too, that fundraising work should remain just one aspect of a music librarian's job. If the librarian enjoys fundraising more than anything else and wants to spend most of the time on this kind of work, a career change may be in order.

We should also be sensitive to the manner in which fundraising can alter the relationship between librarians and library users. Most music library donors are current or past library users who enjoy and respect music librarians for their musical knowledge and expertise in librarianship. But what happens when music librarians, especially those who show skill and interest in fundraising, take on increasing fundraising responsibilities? While this work assists the development office, it could tarnish the relationship between librarian and user. If possible, librarians should retain a distance between themselves and certain fundraising work, especially direct solicitation for money. The librarian may consult privately with the development officer about donors and donations, but it is usually best for the development staff to make the direct ask. Let the development staff also write the planned giving documents and other legal contracts. This removes librarians from direct negotiations and preserves their status as librarians who also raise money rather than fundraisers who also run a library. The librarian in the latter role will lose the trust and respect of library users who might feel that they are being manipulated rather than served. If librarians ever feel uncomfortable or awkward in a fundraising setting, their instincts are probably telling them that is time to back away and let the development staff take over. The librarian should never jeopardize a relationship with any user for the sake of raising money.

INSTITUTIONAL POLITICS

Concealed within a successful fundraising effort may be another even more subtle ramification to consider: jealousy that can arise among library staff members within the institution. This phenomenon is often overlooked, and it may never be an issue at your library, but it can occur. What if the music librarian tells fellow library workers or institutional colleagues about the music library's receipt of impressive donations intended for new collection acquisitions, equipment, staffing, or even a renovation or new building? Staff members who work in other libraries or departments on campus that have not been active or successful in raising money may react with envy and resentment. After all, they ask, why is the music library getting new furniture when their library or department has been requesting new chairs for years? Bad feelings are exacerbated when these same staff members receive additional work, such as cataloging or processing, to support the music library's fundraising efforts. Some individuals may also think that fundraising is inappropriate behavior for library staff, feeling that such work should be conducted by development staff only. It is best to deal with potentially hard feelings quickly rather than letting them stew over time. To face the issue head on, the music librarian could offer to meet with other library staff in order to explain how fundraising works for the music library and how it may succeed in other libraries or departments. The music librarian could even offer to assist the other libraries with writing proposals or other kinds of development work. This collegial approach will give others the opportunity to either attempt fundraising work or decide against it. In either case, this tactic should placate any resentment by allowing library staff to make their own choice. Such meetings will probably need approval from the library administration and development office to be sure that the library can indeed support more fundraising activities.

Library staff members should realize that library and development personnel can try to attract donors to support certain proposals and areas of interest but that they cannot control which projects donors ultimately choose to support. As Anne Ruggiero, director of development for the Center for Health and Community and the Institute for Global Health, University of California, San Francisco, and Julia Zimmerman, dean of libraries at Ohio University, point out, "Donor intent, not administrators' capriciousness, is the engine that drives philanthropy. Sharing biographical information or anecdotes about the donor with staff or describing the donor's decision-making process can ameliorate misplaced fears."[2] Communicating in this manner may also point out that there is a certain amount of luck that goes along with the hard work involved in attracting donors to library projects.

Music libraries with successful fundraising programs, as well as those music libraries hoping to expand fundraising endeavors, could face scrutiny from their university central development office or other upper-level administration. This situation does not involve jealousy, but rather a concern that the music library could siphon money away from other subject areas or initiatives in need of funding. Such a perspective is more likely to be prevalent in conservatories and smaller college settings in which the music library's donations could represent a sizable percentage of the institution's overall fundraising totals. A music librarian in this position must make a persuasive case to convince administrators that the music library should be a high priority in the institution's quest for fundraising dollars. Without upper administrative support, even a flourishing music library fundraising operation may need to restrict fundraising work, becoming a victim of its own success. Although it can be difficult to accept this fact, the music librarian must always recognize the larger fundraising goals of its institution. While it may be tempting to ignore authority and work around the system in search of fundraising money, such defiance is short-sighted and politically unwise. Librarians should not cross this boundary if they want to carry out fundraising over time. It is best to work within the rules of the organization while pushing the music library fundraising goals as aggressively as possible.

Some music libraries may find themselves in a struggle to survive university-wide reorganizations due to financial reductions and the rethinking of traditional library services. Specialized libraries, especially separate branches, can be especially vulnerable when a library administration looks to reduce costs and consolidate library spaces. A library's chances of survival may improve if it is active and successful in fundraising. A steady stream of donated money allows the library to achieve a certain independence and influence that it might not otherwise enjoy. Added funding improves services and collections, thus strengthening a library's standing on campus. In addition, administrators may have few options when it comes to restructuring a library that raises money. For instance, named library space can be difficult or impossible to alter. Not many library directors would want to inform donors that the music library space they paid millions of dollars to build was converted into an espresso bar. Similarly, donors contribute endowed money according to certain stipulations that the library accepts to honor in perpetuity. Donors may also establish staffing positions that library administrators cannot alter. By raising money successfully, music libraries can better position themselves strategically within their organization. It is a subtle but significant side-benefit of fundraising that music librarians should not overlook.

In spite of its rewards, fundraising can become detrimental to the best interests of a music library if it interferes with essential elements of the library functions. The library should never fall into the trap of raising money just for its own glory without carefully considering its benefits to the library. Keep in mind, too, that the goals of the development office may not always match those of the music library staff. What happens, for example, when a donor offers to contribute a vast amount of money to a project that will take a great deal of music library staff time but result in few, if any, benefits to the library? The development staff may encourage this donation in order to bring in the dollars. After all, development staff members must raise money to keep their jobs. The music librarian will need to resist the donation or change its conditions so that it provides actual rewards for the library. Donations must always have a positive outcome for both the donor and library.

As mentioned earlier in the book, library staff members sometimes question whether it is appropriate for a library to conduct fundraising at all. They argue that librarians are not in the business of making money. They are not trained or paid to solicit funding. For this reason, some librarians have no interest in fundraising and may even consider it to be unscrupulous and disreputable for librarians to raise money. While such an opinion may sound noble and idealistic, it does not acknowledge the ways in which librarians' roles have changed over time. In recent years, library administrators' job descriptions increasingly include fundraising responsibilities. Many academic librarians now seek external funding as part of their operational goals. It is no longer assumed that the library's central budget will pay for all expenses; grants and outside donations are essential in fulfilling a library's needs. For better or worse, fundraising is an integral source of libraries' incomes. By neglecting fundraising work, music librarians may actually deny the full possibilities that could occur within their libraries. One could argue that it is negligent *not* to advocate for some sort of library fundraising efforts. Without fundraising, a library could fall behind its peers that actively seek outside financial support.

No matter how well the music librarian attempts to follow the rules and procedures of fundraising, there will be bumps along the road: there is no acknowledgement for a certain donor at a fundraising event, a thank-you letter describes the wrong gift, or the librarian forgets to copy a donor's manager in an e-mail message. As hard as the music librarian tries to follow fundraising etiquette and procedures, there are many opportunities for mistakes. The goal is to avoid any major blunders which could cost the library or university a sizeable donation or even destroy a relationship with a donor. When mistakes occur, it is best to recognize the errors and check in immediately with a development officer. Besides the fundraising skills of the librarian, the success of fundraising also depends upon the professionalism and experience of development staff connected to the music library. Their support and understanding will be critical at such times. By working together, a mutual respect should develop over time and development staff will acknowledge occasional errors as part of the fundraising process.

ETHICAL CONCERNS

Raising money for music libraries can have enormous rewards, but when money becomes a motivating factor in making decisions, circumstances can present ethical and philosophical issues that may challenge one's fundamental values. Fundraising with individual donors, in particular, can sometimes raise certain ethical concerns for the music librarian. Professional fundraising organizations have taken ethics seriously by creating written codes that address these issues.

The Association of Fundraising Professionals, the Association for Healthcare Philanthropy, the Council for Advancement and Support of Education, and the Giving Institute have created a Donor Bill of Rights, which presents ten guiding principles that are intended to protect donors and provide them with the opportunity to clarify and improve their giving decisions.[3] These philanthropic organizations provide additional rules of behavior to promote proper ethical conduct on the part of their membership.[4] On the library side, the American Library Association has its own Code of Ethics that recognizes the dilemmas and conflict of values that can occur in providing information and intellectual freedom.[5] This code covers general issues but not areas specific to fundraising. The Music Library Association does not have an ethics code for its membership. To inform donors of their policies on giving, several universities include various kinds of donor bill of rights on their development page websites.

Fundraising can sometimes involve situations quite remote from the training and experience of a music librarian. There may be no clear-cut right or wrong answers to some fundraising issues, making the librarian feel uncomfortable and tentative about an appropriate response. When dealing with such grey areas, Marilyn Fischer, associate professor of philosophy at the University of Dayton, recommends that fundraisers ask themselves how their decision will impact upon three factors: their organization's mission, their relationships with the people involved in the situation, and their own personal values and integrity.[6] If an action causes a negative response in any of these areas, the librarian should realize that the initial decision is not appropriate. Remember these factors when considering moral dilemmas that could take place in a music library.

One basic principle of libraries is to provide fair and equal access to their users. This does not necessarily mean equal access for all. Academic music libraries usually provide their university community with privileges that they deny to outside users. However, it is essential that the library staff be consistent in its application of these regulations. With this in mind, librarians should not favor certain users just because of their giving potential. Librarians do not serve their users for the purpose of making a profit or obtaining gifts. It is not appropriate for a librarian to view users as merely potential donors. Librarians are not salespeople and the service they provide their users should have nothing to do with anyone's giving capacity. Throughout the fundraising process, the music librarian should remain sensitive to this issue and be wary of ways in which fundraising could affect library services. Fortunately, most individual donors targeted by the music library will be alumni who enjoyed their time in the library as students, have moved on in life, and now wish to pay back the school and library. They usually are not looking for any services or special benefits from their gifts.[7] The library welcomes these donations and the alumni take pleasure in supporting the library. This is a positive experience for both participants.

But what happens when a library donor attempts to bend these regulations in order to gain certain library privileges? Library staff may feel pressured to make exceptions in order to please the donor. What if a major donor who just contributed $500,000 to the library comes to the library and asks to check a music score out of the library? The library's policy states explicitly that an outside user such as this donor does not have circulation privileges. In this case, however, it may be difficult and even embarrassing to say no. On the other hand, what if the person asking to check out a music score is a donor who contributed $10 to the library? Does the size of the gift dictate the number of privileges the library will grant? If so, by how much? How does this correspond to the library's policies concerning fair application of rules and regulations? The library staff may want to seek advice from the library administration and development office in sorting out such questions. Remember, however, that the development staff may be in favor of bending the rules in order to obtain more gifts. The music librarian can often feel caught in the middle under these circumstances.

Donors may make demands that go against other library policies. A gift in kind with strings attached—that is, specific stipulations—is often not worth accepting. For example, if a donor offers to give a highly prized collection of music manuscripts to the library under the condition that the library must bind them in leather, house them in a special room, and make them accessible only on Tuesdays, the library would certainly refuse the gift even though the scores could strengthen the collection and bring prestige to the university. But what if the stipulations were less absurd and just a slight exception to library regulations would obtain this esteemed collection? How far does the library bend the rules?

Monetary offers from donors can alter the makeup of a library collection and even the school's curriculum. Consider the scenario in which a donor is willing to give $50,000 to the library. This sounds fantastic, except for the donor's stipulation that the library must spend the entire donation to purchase Swedish music. The library has nothing against Swedish music, but it is not part of the music department's curriculum. The library's collection development policy makes no mention of collecting in this area. The library might need to reject this offer unless the donor is willing to alter the donation agreement to include a wider geographic range of music. But what if the library accepts the gift, and later the music department decides to teach a course on Swedish music due to the extraordinarily rich library resources that were purchased with this gift? The donor will alter the music curriculum through this donation. Music librarians need to guard against donors using their money to spread their influence. Even a small donation of $500 or $1000 over several years could transform the shape of a collection. The effect of a donor's influence can even extend well beyond the library and music department. As Kathleen S. Kelly, professor in the Department of Communication at University of Southwestern Louisiana, points out: "It may also be hypothesized that if an institution of higher education loses a high degree of departmental autonomy to external donors, the total institution will eventually suffer by losing control over its power to set and pursue its own goals."[8] While accepting all gifts may be tempting, the library should consider the problematic consequences of certain donations.

Another potential moral dilemma could be the relationship that develops between donor and librarian. Librarians may hold political or philosophical views that are diametrically opposite those of prospective donors. Imagine a librarian going to dinner with a promising prospect who insists on talking about politics, religion, or philosophies that vehemently clash with the librarian's personal views. What if that same donor had also earned millions of dollars in a manner that offends the moral conscience of the librarian? Does the librarian ingratiate himself to this person all in the name of raising money for the library? For a $10 donation, perhaps not. But what if the donor is willing to donate $10 million to the library? The librarian's personal opinions may pale in significance when compared to the countless benefits such a donation would bring to the library and its users. Should librarians subjugate their own views in order to please donors and obtain donations? If so, at what price? Or should librarians remain steadfast to their beliefs no matter how much money a donor dangles in front of them? There are no simple answers to these questions, but they demonstrate another kind of personal conflict that the librarian could encounter in a fundraising context.

It goes without saying that the library staff should never benefit from any personal gifts that involve fundraising. With this in mind, librarians may find themselves in a possible conflict of interest when dealing with gifts in kind. The librarian who makes selection decisions for donated materials must be careful not to let personal collecting interests interfere with the library's collection needs. When the library receives gifts in kind, the music selector will decide which items to keep for the library and which to sell or give away. Of course, it would be unethical for selectors to reject certain materials so that they could take them for themselves. It is unlikely that librarians would make such a choice, but their judgment could be unconsciously swayed if library staff members are able to purchase or take discarded items. To remove any questions, selectors should simply pledge never to obtain any donated items for personal use. This policy makes the selection process cleaner and eradicates any suggestion that selectors might profit personally from a donation.

Lurking behind a successful fundraising effort is another unsettling question: Will a library that raises money receive less funding in its annual library budget? As university and library administrators pinch pennies and stretch diminishing budgets, they might be tempted to allocate less money to those libraries with fundraising incomes. Administrators should recognize the unfairness of this approach and the demoralizing effect it would have on fundraisers. Librarians raising money should be attentive to any disparities in their annual library budgets and be sure that they receive their equitable share of library funding. If the library suspects that a shortfall in its annual budget may be a result of fundraising efforts, the library staff should challenge the fairness of such budgetary prestidigitation.

These are just some of the ethical issues that can emerge in library fundraising. Such moral concerns often fall outside of the usual academic education of librarians. Perhaps the most important guideline to remember is that music librarians should never pursue any fundraising activities unless they are completely comfortable with the ethics of each opportunity. Fundraising should be a positive activity for both library staff and donors. Once an endeavor makes either side uneasy, the library should reassess the process and seriously question whether to continue in that direction.

CONCLUSION

Fundraising presents its share of challenges, but the rewards can be well worth the effort. For those music librarians who have not attempted development activities, there could be a vast unexplored resource of individual donors and grantmaking organizations waiting to hear about the music library's needs and eager to contribute towards a cause in which they believe. Money really is there for the asking. Music librarians are fortunate to work in a discipline that engenders a positive image with donors. For some alumni, the music library holds a special place for them that is worthy of their support. This is not to say that fundraising will be easy or that there is not fierce competition for fundraising dollars from within the university community and beyond. There are also philosophical and ethical concerns to address if we want fundraising to coexist comfortably within the realm of music librarianship.

Music librarians will need to adjust their approach to fundraising according to their own circumstances. Some institutions have well-funded development offices with adequate staffing to assist a music library and its fundraising needs. Other organizations may not have as much emphasis on fundraising, in which case the music library will work more autonomously. The size and type of academic setting (public/private, liberal arts, conservatory, etc.), along with the financial means of its alumni, will determine the potential for fundraising success. The mission statements of the institution and its library system also affect how much support the music library will receive in its own development efforts, as will the senior administration's view of the music library in the total library fundraising design. The music librarian must first sell the idea of fundraising to the appropriate institutional administrators before approaching potential donors or writing grants. Fluctuating economic conditions will also influence the success of fundraising from year to year. In all cases, fundraising will take time, persistence, and a strong commitment from the entire music library staff along with support from library and development colleagues on campus. During the initial stages of this work, donations may be slow to appear, but they should increase steadily over time. Along with these financial rewards will come added staff responsibilities. Fundraising should always fit within a library's priorities and result in tangible benefits to library users.

Music library fundraising allows donors the opportunity to support a meaningful cause that enriches the lives of library users for many years to come. In addition to the satisfaction of giving, donors receive public recognition and often a tax break as well. The library succeeds by obtaining financial support for materials or activities that may not have been possible otherwise. The horizons of a library expand, often significantly, through these donations. The donor and library both win. Music librarians resigned to the status quo may sound like the Rolling Stones in concluding that "you can't always get what you want." The more enterprising librarians among us will find that by tapping into the rich potential of fundraising, you may get much more than you could ever expect.

Appendix 1

CASE STUDIES FROM THE MIT LEWIS MUSIC LIBRARY

LIBRARY RENOVATION

The Rosalind Denny Lewis Music Library traces its history back to 1950 when the Charles Hayden Memorial Library building opened. At that time, music materials were pulled out of the general collection to be housed separately, and the Music Library—really a music lounge and a small library collection—was established as a branch library. By the early 1990s, this library suffered from overflowing shelves, insufficient listening and study space, and inadequate staff space. Other libraries on campus faced similar space issues, but there was no funding available to renovate any of these library spaces. Fundraising would be the only hope for renovating the Music Library.

The music librarian obtained permission in 1994 to create floor plans for a new music library, but without money to support such work. An undergraduate architecture student volunteer drafted some initial plans as part of a class project; a local architectural firm worked pro bono to provide two sets of floor plans along with architectural sketches of the library. One option, a basic reorganization of the floor plan, suggested renovations to improve study and shelf space. The library would be more comfortable and attractive, but without additional space. A more ambitious plan included a mezzanine level that took advantage of the building's double-height first floor. This plan included a media center, private study rooms, staff offices, compact shelving, a special collections room, a recording studio, and an open study area. The cost was about double the amount of the first option.

The architectural plans and estimated budgets were presented at a meeting of library and MIT administrators. Ellen T. Harris, MIT professor of music and then associate provost for the arts, was one of the attendees and greatly interested in the project. She soon located an alumnus who wanted to support the renovation and who preferred the more expensive plan which included the second floor. Melanie Brothers, the architect and project manager of the renovation, worked closely with library staff in designing a space that would offer both beauty and function. Renovation work began during the summer of 1996 when workers emptied and gutted the music library space. To cover mounting building costs, the development officer working with the associate provost found additional donors. Rooms in the new space presented attractive naming opportunities for donors, and alumni contributed money to name the special collections room, media center, and conference room. Composer and MIT professor of music John Harbison added an engaging musical touch to the library's architecture by writing a nineteen-measure canon for the library, entitled *Veni Creator Spiritus*, which adorns the nineteen glass panels on the library's mezzanine floor balcony. Fortunately, the primary donor took a hands-off approach toward the renovation; he asked only to name the new library after his mother-in-law, Rosalind Denny Lewis, and he requested that portraits of Ellen T. Harris and Mrs. Lewis hang in the library. He was content to let the architect and library staff work together without his advice.

The attractive new library, with its second floor and inviting new features, opened in October 1996 as the Rosalind Denny Lewis Music Library. The MIT Libraries paid a small portion of expenses, mostly moving and storage costs, but individual donors funded the renovation almost exclusively. To honor them, the names of the principal donors appear on a plaque in the library. All donors were invited to a gala library opening and reception. This renovation expanded facilities and services, totally transforming the old space. The Lewis Music Library gained a new vitality in a rejuvenated space made possible by helpful volunteers, a supportive music professor, and generous alumni.

LIBRARY NEWSLETTER

The Music Library started a newsletter in 1980 to announce library news, recent acquisitions, and donations. Music faculty, MIT staff, and a few donors were its primary target audience. The newsletter's paper format served as the most effective method of wide-spread communication in the days before the internet and e-mail. In 1994, the name of the newsletter changed to *What's the Score?*, the physical format increased in size, and the library began to issue both paper and online versions of the newsletter. As electronic forms of communication became more prominent, the library sent increasing numbers of e-mails to faculty and staff concerning practical library issues. In turn, the newsletter began to emphasize donations and donors in favor of library news. One of the features of the newsletter had been a list of selected new library acquisitions, including books, scores, videos, and audio recordings. Over the years, this listing took up increasing space in the newsletter, which grew to sixteen pages. By 2007, the newsletter settled on a four-page format and eliminated new acquisition citations because of their ready online accessibility.

Music Library staff produced the newsletter with help from student assistants. The appearance of the newsletter steadily improved over the years. In 2008, the MIT Libraries' Development Office hired a graphic artist who worked with the library staff in redesigning the newsletter to give it a more polished and professional look. The enhanced appearance included more color and graphics by incorporating a preprinted paper "shell" containing banners and photos that remain the same for each issue. Several different issues of the newsletter can be printed on the same shell, thus saving staff time and money. The mailing list of the newsletter increased over the years to include names of those who donated money or gifts in kind to the library or who requested to receive the newsletter; it currently exceeds five hundred names, most of whom are alumni. Because the newsletter functions primarily as a fundraising vehicle, the library still produces the paper version because of its appeal to donors. On-campus library users receive more specific library news through electronic means, such as e-mails, blogs, and Facebook announcements.

Certain features of the newsletter remain over the years, such as the "Bad Jokes" section of four or five short music jokes (viola jokes frequently appear, but the newsletter spares no instrument). The corny nature of these jokes is perhaps their charm. Such humor also conveys a message that the library does not take itself too seriously, and some readers even go to that section first. Another consistent part of the newsletter is the listing of donors' names. The name of every donor who contributes money or gifts in kind appears in the newsletter unless they request not to be acknowledged in print. Significant gifts will merit an article and sometimes a photograph. Most donors appreciate this recognition. As with any acknowledgement, it is essential to recognize all donors. Be sure to assemble the donor list carefully; unintentionally leaving out a name could offend a donor. Several years ago, the music librarian learned the consequences of omitting just one donor's name. Shortly after the release of the music library newsletter, a donor walked into the music librarian's office to ask why his name had been omitted from the gift list. It seemed to be a minor issue, but the donor took the omission quite personally. Of course, the gift was duly noted in the following newsletter, but the music library now takes care to list all donors' names. In fact, this experience prompted the newsletter to include a disclaimer after the listing of donors that states: "If we have inadvertently omitted your name from this list, please contact us!"

In addition to announcing donations, general news items still appear in the newsletter to highlight library activities and new initiatives. Photos of concerts or events in the library also remind readers of the library's connection to the MIT community. Library staff spends considerable time in the writing, production, and distribution of this newsletter. In order to avoid errors and omissions, individuals within the MIT Libraries' system, including development, publicity, and administrative staff, proofread the newsletter before it circulates. This helps to avoid possible political fallout and often results in helpful editorial advice as well. In spite of the work to produce the newsletter, the positive response from donors makes it worth the effort.

CLASS OF 1982 MUSIC LIBRARY FUND

To celebrate its tenth reunion, MIT's Class of 1982 chose the Music Library as one of its areas to support on campus. At first, the number and amount of donations to the library were relatively small. The library provided stewardship by sending donors prompt thank-you letters and acknowledging their gifts in the Music Library and MIT Libraries newsletters. Fortunately, the Class of 1982 Music Library Fund was established as an unrestricted fund so that the library can spend the money on whatever it needs, including equipment and staffing. This type of fund provides the library with a great deal of flexibility.

The first major use of funding from the Class of 1982 was a renovation of the Music Library's media room in 1994. This room housed audio and video equipment on tables in a cramped and dimly lit space. The Music Library's budget was insufficient to enhance the room, but the Class of 1982 fund had accumulated enough money to paint the room, install better lighting, and provide comfortable carrels. This work extensively upgraded the space at a reasonable cost. The library informed donors about this transformation through thank-you notes and newsletter announcements.

Since that project, the library has spent the Class of 1982 funding to improve the library in ways that would not have been possible otherwise. For example, the library purchased an iPad within a week of its initial release in April 2010. This iPad became one of the first iPads to circulate from any library. Our library gained instant attention as blogs picked up the story of circulating iPads in academic libraries. E-mails and phone calls came in from other libraries asking about our experience. Our users were pleased to be the first to use an iPad, and the library received positive publicity for a small price. The library used Class of 1982 money again to purchase an iPad 2 on the first day of its release in March 2011. This funding allows the library to purchase items quickly and without administrative red tape.

In 2009, the Class of 1982 funded another small renovation. The library's media center consisted of approximately thirty listening and viewing stations that were housed in large custom-built carrels. Built in 1996, these stations were enormously popular in the days before iPods, laptops, and electronic reserves. In fact, the library set up waiting lists for these stations during busy times of the semester. Use of the media center declined steadily as the need for playback equipment dwindled, and by 2008, the library's media center resembled a ghost town. An update was needed, but the timing for this project could not have been worse—donors were hard to find during the financial downturn, and the MIT Libraries' budget could not support this work. Once again, the library turned to the Class of 1982 fund for help. The library rehired the architect of the library's 1996 renovation for this much smaller project. She provided invaluable advice and designed two spacious, custom-built wooden tables to replace sixteen listening carrels. These tables hold computers with music notational software, and they also serve for general study where students bring their laptops and spread out their work. This renovation included new ceiling lighting as well. Thanks to this work, the library's media center is attracting students once again.

Over the years, the Class of 1982 Fund also purchased various pieces of audiovisual equipment for the library, ranging from television monitors to iPods. One year, the library had spent its annual collections budget when a faculty member requested that the library obtain the first twenty-three volumes from a new edition of Carl Nielsen's complete works. Fortunately, the Class of 1982 Fund had the money needed to purchase this set. Another time, the MIT Museum offered the library a massive photograph, measuring six feet by eight feet, of the MIT Banjo Club from 1893. The challenge to accepting this gift was that this striking photo lacked a frame and needed to be wall mounted. Once more, the Class of 1982 provided the necessary funding to undertake this project quickly.

Stewardship of the Class of 1982 members results in faithful and increasingly generous donations to the library. Class members trust that the library spends their money in timely and creative ways. The music librarian communicates to all Class of 1982 donors through thank-you letters and its newsletter. The Lewis Music Library also maintains a web page that illustrates the many ways in which the Class of 1982 supports the library (http://libraries.mit.edu/music/donations/class1982.html). Without such stewardship over the years, donations to this fund may have diminished or disappeared altogether.

A few members of this class occasionally return to MIT and visit the library during reunions or other events on campus. Class members see firsthand the ways in which their funding improves the library. Such visits strengthen connections to the library and personal bonds to the staff. Class reunions provide a good reason for the library to contact these donors and invite them back to the library for tours and conversation. Personal contact is the best way to establish and strengthen relationships with donors. If possible, contact the administrative officers of these classes, such as class president, secretary, or treasurer, and reintroduce them to your library. They know their classmates well, and they may be willing to recruit additional names to support the library.

MITSO RECORDINGS

David Epstein (1930–2002) conducted the MIT Symphony Orchestra (MITSO) from 1965 to 1998. During that time, he inspired generations of students who learned both musical and life lessons as part of the orchestra. The orchestra made memorable tours, and it even issued commercial recordings—no small feat for an orchestra of mostly engineering students with a passion for music. Many MITSO alumni still have warm feelings towards Dr. Epstein and their experiences in MITSO. Upon his retirement, Dr. Epstein donated several hundred reel-to-reel tapes of his MITSO recordings to the Lewis Music Library. After his death, his widow donated even more reel-to-reel tapes to the library. Unfortunately, the outdated format of these valuable recordings was incompatible with the library's public listening stations. Without funding to reformat the tapes, the library was faced with the possibility of having to store them off campus, where they would slowly deteriorate and probably not be heard again.

In listening to the high quality of these performances and remembering the fondness of the MITSO alumni toward David Epstein, the music librarian hoped to reformat these tapes onto CD and make them available to the MIT community. However, the library's budget could not pay for these transfers, so the music librarian mentioned the project to development staff in hopes of raising money from donors. Fortunately, the development officer working for the music department generously provided the library with names of alumni who had performed in MITSO, along with permission to contact these individuals. An alumna from the orchestra, along with the music librarian, wrote letters to thirty of the most promising prospects as well as emails to a few hundred more alumni of the orchestra. Within three months, the MITSO alumni had funded the entire project with donations totaling over $50,000! The library outsourced the audio reformatting work to a local recording engineer who had worked with David Epstein over the years. A graphic artist designed the CD covers and liner notes, which include Epstein's program notes along with the names of the performers. The library's music cataloger solved metadata issues and cataloged the CDs. It took longer than expected to complete this work, but after approximately two years, the project transferred seventy-two concerts to CD format. These CDs allow listeners who enter the library to enjoy performances that document a piece of MIT music history. The donors are pleased with the project, and some of them have become annual supporters of the Lewis Music Library.

In 2011, music library staff improved access to the MITSO audio recordings even further. Selected MITSO performances of compositions published before 1923 (to comply with copyright law) are now available through MIT TechTV, an open-source video repository. Listeners from around the world can enjoy these performances over the internet. This service was made possible by the MITSO alumni who allowed the library to digitize the original tape recordings and save them from extinction. The music library plans to promote this new accessibility of MITSO to the alumni and possibly contact them to support other fundraising projects in the future.

ORAL HISTORY PROJECT

One benefit of working in a music library is the opportunity to associate with a variety of musicians. One day in 1998, a particularly spirited conversation took place at the Music Library's circulation desk between a retired music faculty member and Forrest Larson, the library's circulation and reserves assistant. The professor reminisced about his career throughout the world and mentioned his work with other musicians such as Béla Bartók, Zoltán Kodály, and George Szell. After the professor left, Forrest and the music librarian regretted that they had not recorded the conversation. They had talked about oral history before, but this conversation inspired them to establish an oral history program in the library. Money was lacking to sponsor such a program, but Forrest began to incorporate some oral history work into his regular job schedule. And so began the Music at MIT Oral History Project in 1999. Forrest conducts in-depth interviews with retired music faculty, staff, and former students, who share their reflections and knowledge of music at MIT. Furthermore, their professional lives and activities are often historically important to the world at large. Forrest would record the interview on DAT tape and produce a circulating CD for the library along with a preservation CD copy. The library cataloged each interview and made them available for circulation. With no budget to support this endeavor, there were no written transcripts and not much publicity for the project. Finding time for this work in his busy schedule was not easy for Forrest, but it was a labor of love, so he managed to make progress over time.

From 1999 to 2006, Forrest conducted approximately twenty-five audio interviews, which capture information about music at MIT that is unavailable elsewhere. While the project provided valuable primary-source material, it was still not officially part of Forrest's library work. Things changed in 2006, however, when an alumnus visited the Lewis Music Library with library development staff. As a student at MIT during the 1950s, this alumnus had been actively involved with music. He was considering a gift to MIT, but had not decided where to give it. The music library staff presented him with several possibilities, such as improving the world music collections, reformatting reel-to-reel tape recordings of MIT concerts, and supporting the Music at MIT Oral History project.

The donor liked the oral history project and he soon funded the project so that Forrest could work half-time on this project as an official part his job for at least five years. This funding would also allow the library to create written transcripts of the interviews. The donor later contributed additional funding to provide written transcripts of the project's earlier interviews as well. Forrest relinquished the reserves part of his job, and the library hired a half-time person for that work. The project shifted from audio to video recordings of interviews in the fall of 2010. The video format provides several advantages. The text of the interview scrolls along with the spoken words, and keyword searching allows the viewer to locate specific terms within the interview. These video interviews appear online, providing widespread access through the internet. At the end of 2010, the donor again supported the project by signing a three-year pledge to extend the project even further. This endeavor exists because of the initiative taken by a music library staff member along with a donor's genuine enthusiasm and generous sponsorship of the work.

COLLECTION ENDOWMENT

The Lewis Music Library has a small number of endowed collections funds. One of the oldest funds dates from the 1980s, when a widow created an endowment in honor of her husband who attended MIT and spent many enjoyable hours in the Music Library. This fund purchases the kinds of music that this alumnus enjoyed most. The library collects books, scores, and recordings in these same areas, which support the curriculum and strengthen the collection. Because the donor lives nearby, she occasionally visits the Lewis Music Library. She appreciates the value of her endowment to the library and its significance as a living memorial to her husband.

In recent years, she encouraged friends who knew her husband to contribute to the endowment. These individuals enjoy supporting the cause, and the accumulation of contributions from new donors results in better buying power for the fund. Occasionally, friends of the widow visit from out of town, and they like to visit the Lewis Music Library. The library staff fills a table with a sampling of items purchased through the endowment, including books, scores, CDs, and DVDs. It makes an impressive assortment of materials and reminds everyone of the positive impact that this endowment has on the library's collection. Music faculty members sometimes attend the meetings to explain the value of these materials on their teaching. In this way, donors see firsthand the real impact of their support. In examining these materials at one such visit, the discussion turned to broadening the scope of the endowment to include a wider range of popular music. The suggested subjects are part of the music department's teaching curriculum, so the library readily agreed to collect these other musical styles. Because of close communication with the donor, this endowment now encompasses a broader collecting scope that further enhances the library's collection.

Beginning in July 2010, the MIT Libraries implemented a new process that provides electronic bookplates in catalog records for materials purchased with named funds. Now all materials purchased with such funds, regardless of media, can receive this new type of bookplate. The "e-bookplate," acknowledging the donor or honoree, is a permanent part of the item's catalog record. Not only does this further memorialize the honoree of a fund, but it helps others to recognize the impact of these gifts. Prior to this new process, only books, scores, and other bound materials in the music library received paper bookplates.

Donors have different reasons for establishing endowment funds. Supporters of the Lewis Music Library have an attachment to the library that inspires them to give. Perhaps they were impressed by the library's service and collection while students. They may have fond memories of the library and how music allowed them (or others) to survive the rigors of academic studies. It is not unusual for visiting alumni to tell library staff how the Music Library helped them keep their sanity during their challenging student days. With such strong feelings, alumni enjoy paying the library back for the services it provided. Whatever the reasons, endowments represent the kind of giving that enhances and fulfills both donor and library. Anyone who considers fundraising to be a dirty word should talk to these donors about their experience with endowments and how it helps to enrich their lives.

VIOLIN MUSIC DONATION

Librarians often bristle at the topic of gifts in kind. Libraries regularly receive unwanted material that they must examine and then sell, give away, or throw out. It takes staff time and often provides little return. However, libraries occasionally get lucky. This was the case in 2001 when the Lewis Music Library obtained a donation of 2,680 pieces of violin music from Lois Craig, former associate dean of MIT's School of Architecture and Planning. Her late husband, Stephen Prokopoff, a museum director as well as a fine violinist, assembled this extensive collection from various countries throughout the world over many years. The donation includes a few rare editions and some pieces that were new to the library's holdings, and it emphasizes twentieth-century music, an area that the library wanted to expand. The popularity of chamber music at MIT was another reason to obtain this music. The disadvantage to accepting a gift of this size is the expense to process, bind, catalog, and store the music. Rather than losing this donation to another institution, the music library accepted the gift with the hopes of finding support for it later. The library planned to add these scores to its circulating collection, but it needed money for this to happen.

Funding for this collection appeared in a fortuitous manner. The Council for the Arts at MIT is a campus-wide group that supports arts organizations on campus. In the spring of 2002, a council member met with the music librarian about a grant proposal for library materials to support a new music class on hip-hop. During the discussion, the music librarian mentioned the newly acquired Prokopoff violin donation and its potential value to the MIT community.

The council member was impressed by this collection and shortly sent the Music Library a check that paid to process, bind, and help catalog two thousand pieces of music chosen for the library collection.

To celebrate this gift of violin music along with the contribution that made it accessible, the Lewis Music Library invited MIT students to select music from the donation and perform it in the library. The first Prokopoff Concert in 2003 was an immediate success and the concert is now an ongoing annual tradition. This free concert provides outstanding outreach to the MIT community. It publicly thanks the donors, publicizes the donation, brings people into the library, and acknowledges the library's close connection with students and the music department. Best of all, these violin scores circulate widely, and the library boasts a new depth to a vital part of its collection. Gifts in kind may not always be welcome, but in this case the library's decision to accept the Prokopoff donation is an enduring success in numerous ways.

Appendix 2

DONATION INFORMATION ON SELECTED MUSIC LIBRARY WEBSITES

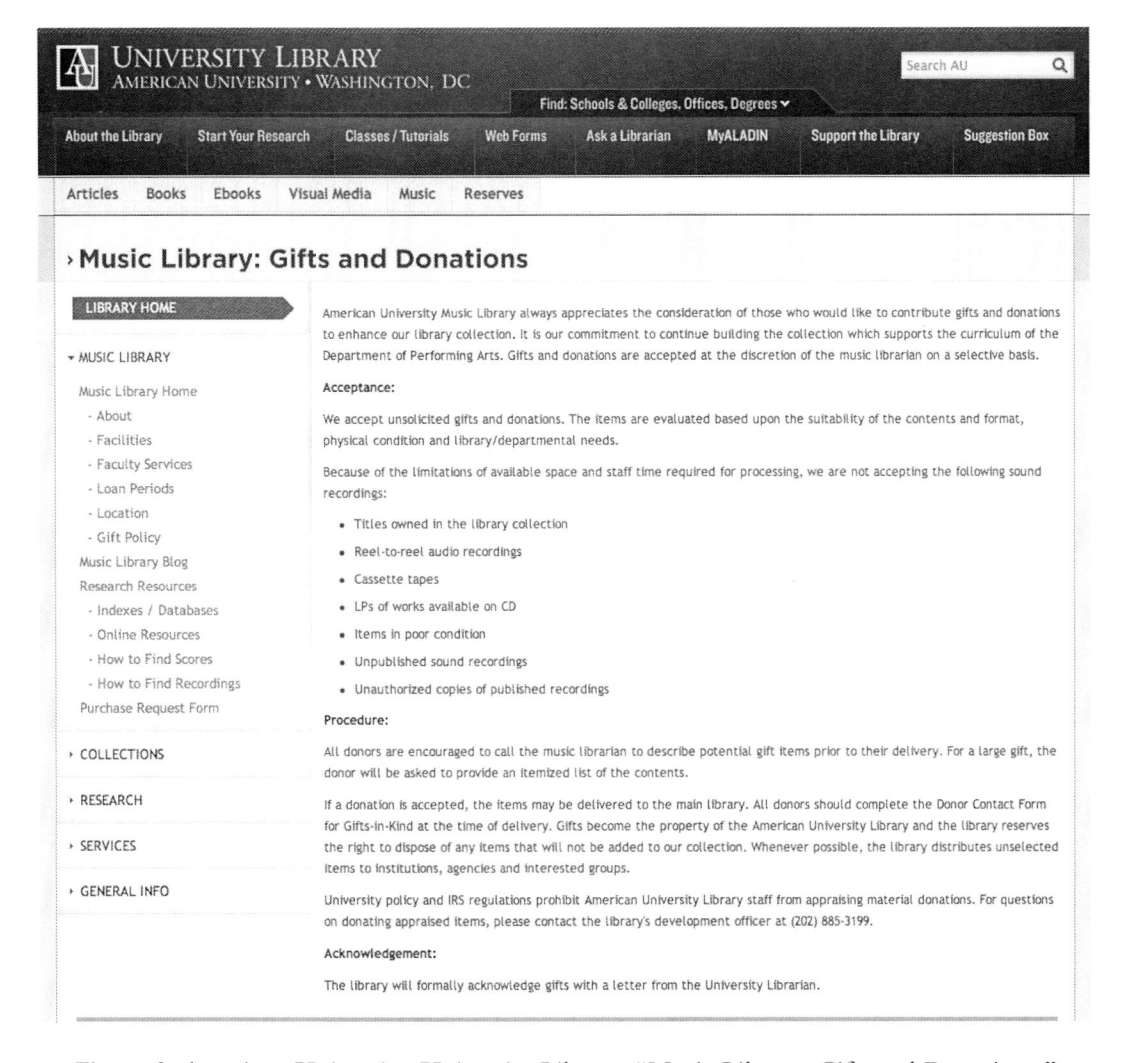

Figure 2. American University, University Library, "Music Library: Gifts and Donations," http://www.american.edu/library/music/gifts.cfm.

Gift Policy for the Music Library

(Updated 8/11)

The Music Library appreciates donations. Please note that these are specialized policies for the Music Library. For general policies, click here.

Donations of music materials are accepted directly at the Music Library. However, **before delivering anything to the Music Library**, please consult the Music Librarian, Maurice Saylor (202-319-5424).

We accept music, sound and printed, encompassing all genres (classical, popular, folk, world, musical theatre, etc.). Items must be in good condition with no evident mold and with all pieces intact. If we decide not to acquire an item, it will be placed in our music sale.

Accepted Formats

- **CDs (compact discs) and DVDs (digital versatile discs)**
- **Musical Scores and Sheet Music**
- **Books**
- **Periodicals** – Periodicals are only accepted upon consultation with the Music Librarian. We generally do not accept common periodicals such as Opera News or other titles which are readily available online.
- **Archival Material** – We encourage donations of materials related to CUA such as programs, photos, recordings, letters, correspondence, etc. We do not accept programs (e.g. opera programs from performances at the Kennedy Center) unless they are CUA-related.
- **Manuscripts** – Manuscripts in great numbers are only accepted upon consultation with the Music Librarian.

Outdated Formats

We no longer accept the following formats (exceptions might be made for Gregorian Chant and items related to CUA):

- Laser Discs (12-inch video discs)
- LPs (Long-Play Records)
- Cassette tapes (audio cassettes)
- Videocassettes (VHS tapes)
- 8-track tapes
- 78s (78 RPM records)

Figure 3. The Catholic University of America, University Libraries, "Gift Policy for the Music Library," part 1. http://libraries.cua.edu/music/gift.cfm.

Equipment

We accept the following in working condition:

- Laser Disc players
- DVD players
- CD players
- LP players (turntables)
- Speakers
- Receivers

We do not accept the following:

- 8-track players
- VHS players (VCRs)
- Televisions
- Beta/Betamax players
- Cassette tape players and dubbers

We may accept certain outdated/older equipment even in non-working condition, such as reel-to-reel players, Moog synthesizers, and players of unusual formats. Please consult the music librarian for more information.

Send questions/comments to the Libraries

Last reviewed: August 16, 2011

Contact Us/Directory | Copyright Information | Speech Enabled   *Celebrating 125 Years*
The Catholic University of America • 620 Michigan Ave., N.E. • Washington, DC 20064

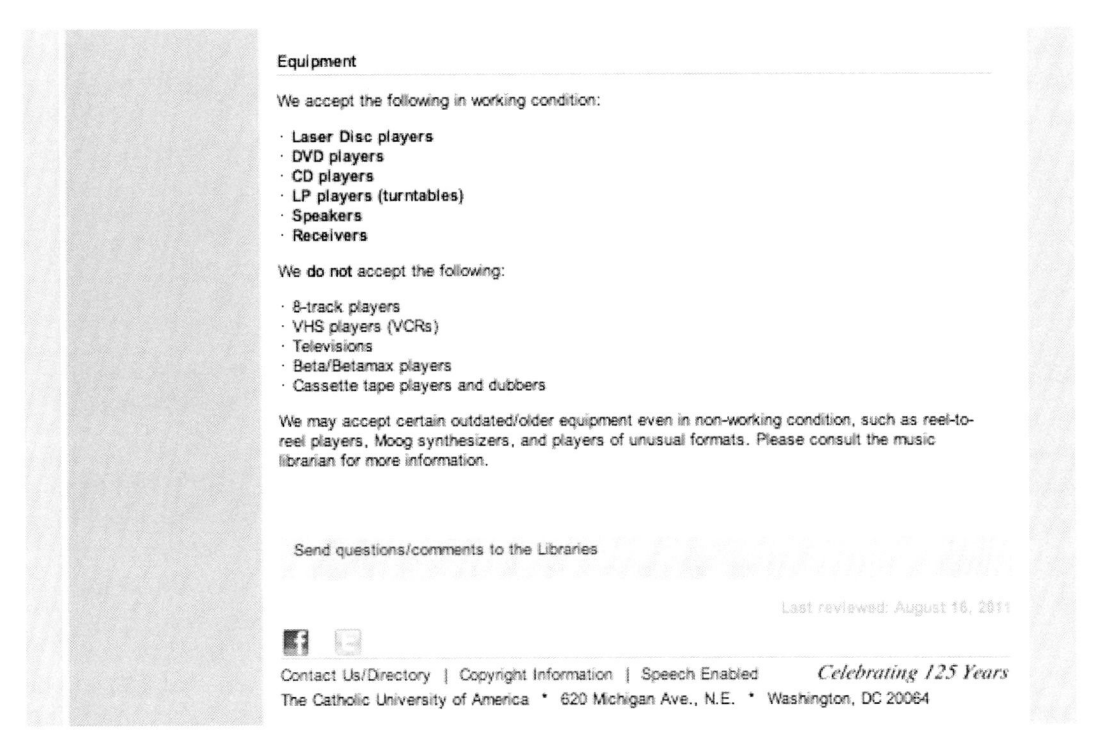

Figure 4. The Catholic University of America, University Libraries, "Gift Policy for the Music Library," part 2. http://libraries.cua.edu/music/gift.cfm.

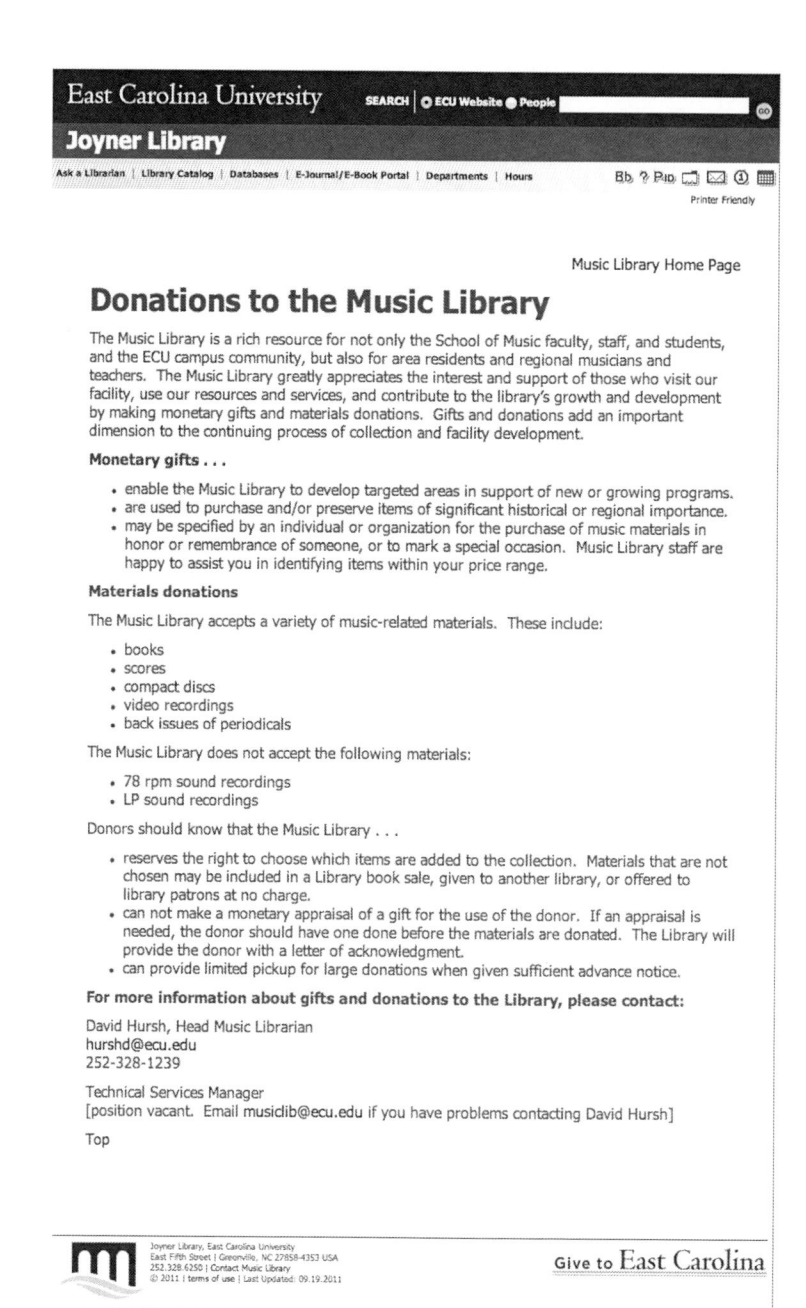

Figure 5. East Carolina University, Joyner Library, "Donations to the Music Library," http://www.ecu.edu/cs-lib/music/donations.cfm.

Figure 6. The Ohio State University, University Libraries, Music and Dance, "Support the Library," http://library.osu.edu/find/collections/music-dance-library/support-the-library.

Queens College Music Library
Aaron Copland School of Music

Home | CUNY+ | Databases | Finding Resources | Services | Exhibits | Staff | Giving

Hours

Monday - Thursday
9:00 am - 7:45 pm

Friday
9:00 am - 4:45 pm

Hours - All Libraries

Quick Resources

Connect from Home
Find Books, CDs, etc. (CUNY+)
Renew Library Materials
Request Books or Scores:
· From Another CUNY Library
· Through Interlibrary Loan
Aaron Copland School of Music
Queens College Libraries
Queens College Home
CUNY Home

Location & Contact

Music Building, Room 225
65-30 Kissena Blvd.
Flushing, NY 11367-1597

(tel) 718-997-3900
(fax) 718-997-3928

Follow us on Facebook

Giving: Support the Library

Go to: Monetary Donations, Endowments, Gifts in Kind, Bequests

Monetary Donations

Private donations from alumni, members of the Queens College community, and the wider community provide much needed support for the Music Library. Donations of any amount are helpful and allow us to purchase more materials for the Music Library collections (such as scores, books on music, recordings, reference materials, facsimiles, etc.). For donations given in honor or memory of someone, we will insert a special bookplate in each donated book with the name(s) of the donor or the honoree, which also be included in the record in the CUNY+, as well as a letter acknowledging the donation.

Anyone who donates $50 or more to the Library is entitled to borrowing privileges for one year. Whether donations are made through the Queens College Foundation (specify for the Music Library) or within the Music Library, donors are asked to consult the Library Circulation Desk in the Benjamin Rosenthal Library at 718-997-3702 to receive their borrowing card.

There are several ways to donate to the Music Library: through the Head of the Music Library or the Queens College Foundation. To give directly to the Music Library, contact Dr. Jennifer Oates for more information (718-997-3901). Visit the Queens College Foundation webpage for Giving Opportunities to make a donation online with a credit card or for additional options.

Back to Top

Endowments

An endowment is a permanent gift that keeps on giving. The principal remains intact and only a percentage of the earned income is used annually by the Music Library. The Music Library has two existing Endowments that can be contributed to:

- David Walker S. Walker Endowment for Music Education
- The Ursula Springer Choral Music Endowment

Additional endowments can be established for as little as $10,000 and can be used to support a subject of interest to the donor. Depending on size, endowments are named after their donors or the ones they wish to honor.

Listed below are some of the subject areas the Music Library hopes to establish endowments for:

- Music theory
- Musicology/music history
- New music (to support the undergraduate and graduate composition programs)
- Performance (further subdivided by division: winds, brass, strings, keyboard, percussion, voice)
- Jazz

Figure 7. Queens College Music Library, [City University of New York], Aaron Copland School of Music, "Giving: Support the Library," part 1, http://qcpages.qc.cuny.edu/Music_Library/giving.php.

If you are interested in establishing an endowment fund or contributing to an existing fund, please contact Dr. Jennifer Oates in the Music Library (718-997-3901) or the Queens College Office of Development, 718-997-3790.

Back to Top

Gifts in Kind: Donating Books, Scores, Recordings, or Music Collections

Many people acquire fine private collections reflecting their professional interests, travel, research and hobbies. We encourage alums, faculty, and members of the community to donate the books, scores, recordings, and other music resources to enrich the Music Library collection and support the growing Aaron Copland School of Music curriculum and the wider CUNY community.

Due to the needs of the Music Library and space constraints, the following materials cannot be accepted:

- books or scores in brittle condition or whose pages are brittle or damaged by water
- material in formats outdated or not collected by the Library (e.g., LPs, audio-books)
- any periodicals (newspapers, magazines, journals, etc.)

All materials donated to the Queens College Libraries become its property. Gift materials not added to the collection may be sold, offered to other libraries, or disposed of at the Library's discretion.

Gifts to the Queens College Libraries are tax-deductible. Please refer to the IRS for its policies on gift giving. Please note that appraisals are solely the responsibility of the donor. Donors considering a tax deduction who wish to have their collection appraised, must do so prior to making the donation because once the gift is received by the Library an appraisal CANNOT be accommodated.

A note in our online catalog will identify each book donated and added to the library's collection. Bookplates will be provided if the requested by the donor. Acknowledgement letters will be sent to the donor.

Please contact Dr. Jennifer Oates for more information (718-997-3901).

Back to Top

Bequests

Individuals may wish to make a deferred gift to the Queens College Library, gift by will, trust, gift annuity, life insurance, real estate, or stocks. Assistance is available for legal and tax questions regarding bequests. Please contact the Queens College Office of Development (718-997-3790).

Figure 8. Queens College Music Library, [City University of New York], Aaron Copland School of Music, "Giving: Support the Library," part 2, http://qcpages.qc.cuny.edu/Music_Library/giving.php.

Figure 9. RCM [Royal College of Music], Library, "Support Us," http://www.rcm.ac.uk/library/supportus/.

Restore a Score
Royal College of Music Library

What you can do to help
There are three ways you can donate to the *Restore a Score* programme:
    a. Pay the full cost of conservation for an item in the RCM Library Collections
    b. Make a donation towards the conservation cost of an item
    c. Make a general donation towards the *Restore a Score* Fund

If you select to make a donation to be associated with a specific item (a. and b. above), then please choose one or more of the items listed below and transfer the reference number and short title – enough to identify it – to the donation form.

Items for conservation
The list below contains items drawn from the RCM Library Collections that currently need conservation treatment. It is by no means exhaustive and we will add to it over the coming months as items receive attention. Many thanks for your generosity.

MANUSCRIPT MUSIC (AUTOGRAPH, UNLESS OTHERWISE STATED)

Composer and work	Cost of conservation	RCM ref. no.
John Barnard: a very important collection of English liturgical music, copied in individual part books between c.1625 and 1638. Barnard, a minor canon of St Paul's Cathedral, used this material as printer's copy for the first collection of church music published in England, *The First Book of Selected Church Musick* (1641). These are among the most heavily used MSS at the RCM and would benefit from further conservation.	£250 per vol. (£2000 in total) £100 donated	MM88
Spohr: *Des Heilands letzte Stunden*. Copyist's full score, inscribed by the composer on at a performance by the Sacred Harmonic Society in London, 5 July 1852. 2 vols. MS 1167	£800	MM87
Music by Great Masters. An important collection of instrumental music from late 17th and early 18th century English theatrical works. 2 vols. (violin & bass parts). MS 1144.	£450	MM 79
Graun: Italian Cantatas. Mid 18th-century copyist's score of works by this important German composer. MS 882	£350	MM77
Hurlstone: *The Magic Mirror*. Full score of orchestral suite based on the story of Snow White and the Seven Dwarfs. 1900. MS 4516	£350	MM 80
John Stafford Smith: *An Introduction to the art of composing Musick*. Composer to the Chapel Royal, Smith was also a well-known antiquarian with a strong interest in the theory of music. 2nd half of the 18th century. MS 2097	£300	MM72
Italian cantata extracts, copied in the late 18th century by the Oxford antiquarian James Malchair. MS 1098	£275	MM68
Bononcini: *L'Astarto*. Mid 18th century copyist's full score, owned by the composer William Shield in 1795. MS 83.	£275	MM78
Dubourg: *Odes*. Autograph full scores of royal birthday odes written by the Master and Composer of State Music in Ireland. Mid 18th century. MS 849	£250	MM84
William Hawes: large collection, in various hands, of glees by this important early 19th century London musician. MS 7001	£225	MM86
Legrenzi: De profundis. 18th-century English copy from Legrenzi's *Sacri e festivi concenti* (1667). MS 930	£200	MM47
Boyce: Odes for the King's Birthday, 1758, and the New Year, 1759. Copied by E.T. Warren in 1760. MS 95.	£200	MM 90
Italian and English sacred vocal music. Late 18th-century collection of vocal music by Italian and English composers, including Croft, Pergolesi and Steffani, used at the Concerts of Ancient Music in London. MS 670	£200	MM 91
Winter: *Il Maometto*. Early 19th century manuscript full score of a two act opera. MS 644	£190	MM 96
Geminiani:: Concerti grossi, op. 4. Contemporary manuscript full score of these popular works, used at the Concerts of Ancient Music. MS 869.	£150	MM 94
Howells: *Motet for Canterbury*. Written for the World Harvest Festival, 1948, MS 4605	£125	MM 92
Howells: *Five Pieces for Organ*. Dedicated to Herbert Sumsion, 1939-40. MS 4611	£125	MM 93
Howells: Magnificat & Nunc Dimittis for St John's College, Cambridge, 1958. Howells was acting organist of St John's College during World War II. MS 4607	£100	MM 95
Hurlstone: *Alfred the Great*: ballad for chorus and orchestra. Vocal score. Hurlstone's sole large-scale choral work.	£100 £25 donated	MM75
Romberg: *Die Kindesmorderin*. Contemporary copyist's manuscript vocal score of a setting of verses by Schiller for soprano solo and chorus. MS 544	£100	MM64

Figure 10. "Restore a Score," Royal College of Music Library, http://www.rcm.ac.uk/supportus/waystosupport/sponsorshipopportunities/restoreascore/Restore%20a%20Score%20-%20Public%20List%20February%202011.pdf.

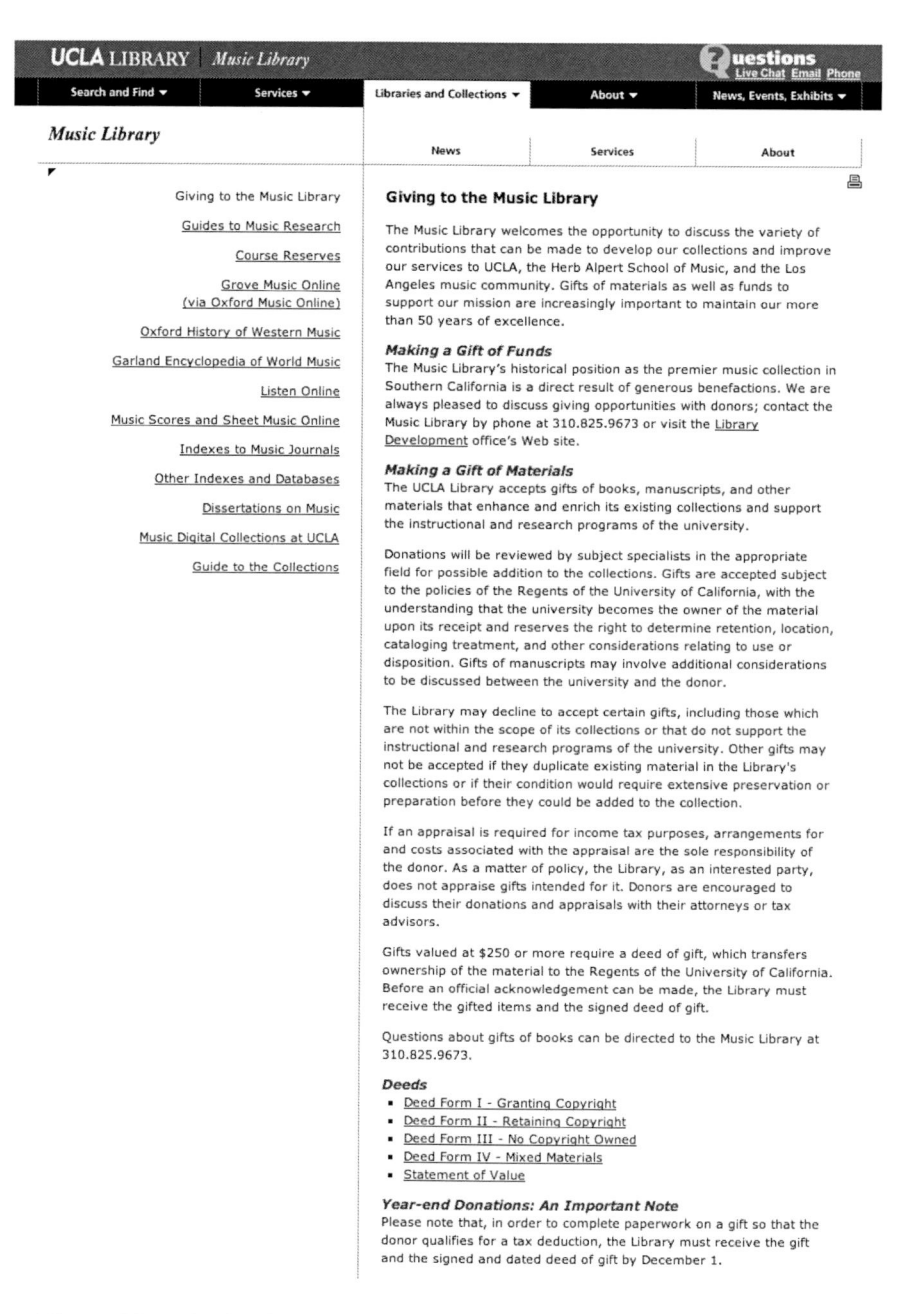

Figure 11. UCLA Library, Music Library, "Giving to the Music Library," http://www.library.ucla.edu/libraries/music/13674.cfm.

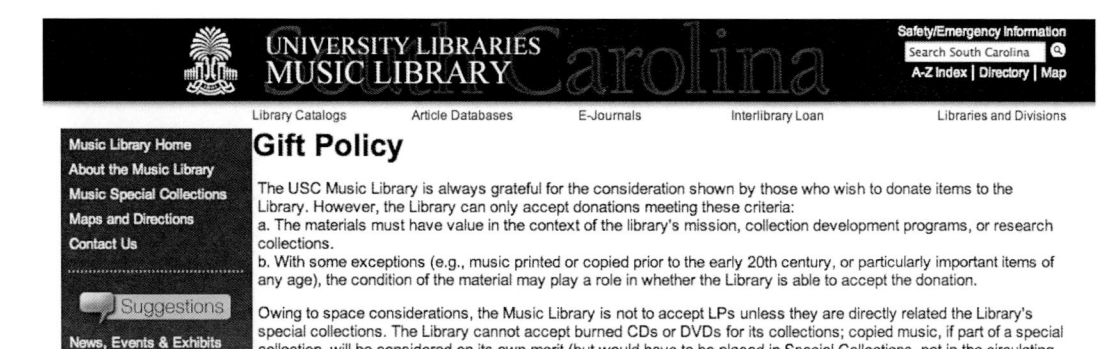

Figure 12. University of South Carolina, University Libraries, Music Library, "Gift Policy." http://library.sc.edu/music/gift_policy.html.

Washington University Libraries

Site Search [ ] Go

Hours | Site Index

? Ask Us
email chat phone text

My Library Accounts | Interlibrary Loan | Reserves

- Library Home
- Search Resources
  - Classic Catalog
  - Discovery Catalog
  - Articles
  - Databases
- Research Help
- News & Events
- How Do I ...
- Services
- Libraries
- Comments
- WUSTL

[Return to Gaylord Music Library Page]

Gaylord Music Library

Donations

The Gaylord Music Library is grateful for the support received through gifts and donations. The Music Library is happy to receive materials in good condition suitable for student use. Materials that are not needed for the collection are regularly offered to music students for their own personal use.

Rare and unique music materials are particularly welcome as well. These materials will likely become part of the Gaylord Music Library Special Collections. Of particular interest are St. Louis (and regional) music publications/recordings as well as materials by well-known area composers and performers.

Making a Gift

If you are interested in making a gift of material to The Gaylord Music Library, please first contact by telephone, U.S. mail, fax, or electronic mail the Music Librarian. Providing a description and/or listing of the item(s) or collection under consideration is very helpful. Information on quantity and condition of material is useful. For printed items, providing us with the author, title, date, publisher or printer, and place of publication is also helpful.

Please send information to:
Brad Short, Music Librarian
Gaylord Music Library

Mailing address:
Campus Box 1061
Washington University in St. Louis
St. Louis, MO 63130-4899

Street address:
6500 Forsyth Blvd.
Clayton, MO 63105

Voice: (314) 935-5529
email: short@wustl.edu

Physical Transfer of Materials and Transfer of Ownership

If you and a member of the Library's collecting staff determine that the Library is the best place for your item(s) or collection, the Library will arrange for delivery of the material to the Gaylord Music Library. Staff members may pack and pick up the material, or request that you pack and send it by U.S. Mail, FedEx, or UPS. Include a brief inventory of the materials being sent, and notify us before making a shipment so that we may be prepared to receive it. Shipments should be made to the following address, as appropriate:

Gaylord Music Library
Washington University in St. Louis
Campus Box 1061
One Brookings Drive
St. Louis MO 63130

A gift agreement outlining the terms and conditions of the donation will be drafted and sent to you for your approval and signature. Our online version can be used as is or customized to suit donors' needs. Upon the receipt of material by Washington University, we will send you a letter acknowledging your gift. The acknowledgement letter or the signed gift agreement is the instrument by which legal ownership is transferred from you to the Gaylord Music Library.

Sample Deed of Gift

Appraisals and Tax Deductions

It is often advantageous to the donor to use a gift of materials to the library as a tax deduction. Please contact your tax advisor to see if your gift requires special IRS forms. If the gift is to be used for tax purposes, often an appraisal is required. The library, being the beneficiary, cannot serve as the appraiser of a gift it is to receive. For a list of local appraisers, please consult your tax advisor or contact the Music Librarian.

For more on gift agreements in general, see the Society of American Archivists brochure "A Guide to Deeds of Gift."

Figure 13. Washington University Libraries, Gaylord Music Library, "Donations," http://library.wustl.edu/units/music/spec/donations.html.

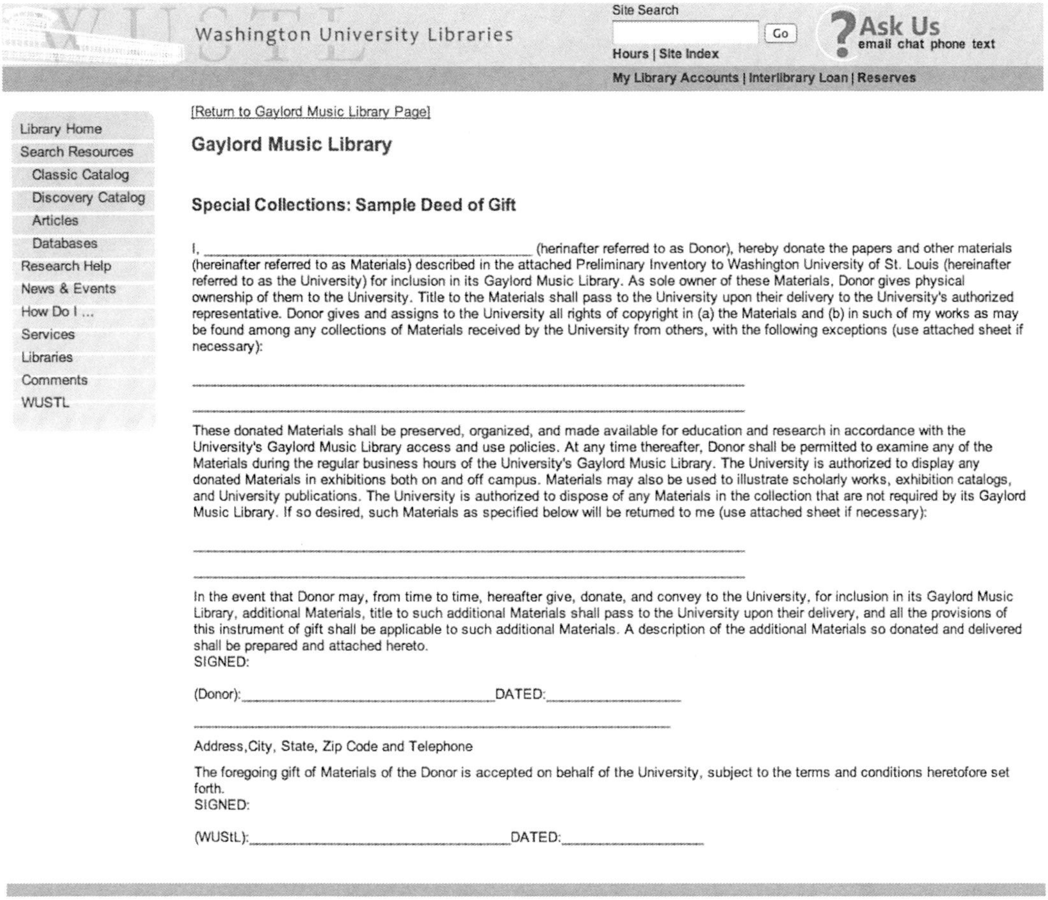

Washington University Libraries

Site Search

Go

Hours | Site Index

Ask Us
email chat phone text

My Library Accounts | Interlibrary Loan | Reserves

Library Home
Search Resources
Classic Catalog
Discovery Catalog
Articles
Databases
Research Help
News & Events
How Do I ...
Services
Libraries
Comments
WUSTL

[Return to Gaylord Music Library Page]

Gaylord Music Library

Special Collections: Sample Deed of Gift

I, ______________________________ (herinafter referred to as Donor), hereby donate the papers and other materials (hereinafter referred to as Materials) described in the attached Preliminary Inventory to Washington University of St. Louis (hereinafter referred to as the University) for inclusion in its Gaylord Music Library. As sole owner of these Materials, Donor gives physical ownership of them to the University. Title to the Materials shall pass to the University upon their delivery to the University's authorized representative. Donor gives and assigns to the University all rights of copyright in (a) the Materials and (b) in such of my works as may be found among any collections of Materials received by the University from others, with the following exceptions (use attached sheet if necessary):

____

____

These donated Materials shall be preserved, organized, and made available for education and research in accordance with the University's Gaylord Music Library access and use policies. At any time thereafter, Donor shall be permitted to examine any of the Materials during the regular business hours of the University's Gaylord Music Library. The University is authorized to display any donated Materials in exhibitions both on and off campus. Materials may also be used to illustrate scholarly works, exhibition catalogs, and University publications. The University is authorized to dispose of any Materials in the collection that are not required by its Gaylord Music Library. If so desired, such Materials as specified below will be returned to me (use attached sheet if necessary):

____

____

In the event that Donor may, from time to time, hereafter give, donate, and convey to the University, for inclusion in its Gaylord Music Library, additional Materials, title to such additional Materials shall pass to the University upon their delivery, and all the provisions of this instrument of gift shall be applicable to such additional Materials. A description of the additional Materials so donated and delivered shall be prepared and attached hereto.
SIGNED:

(Donor):______________________ DATED:____________

____

Address,City, State, Zip Code and Telephone

The foregoing gift of Materials of the Donor is accepted on behalf of the University, subject to the terms and conditions heretofore set forth.
SIGNED:

(WUStL):______________________ DATED:____________

Figure 14. Washington University Libraries, Gaylord Music Library, "Special Collections: Sample Deed of Gift." http://library.wustl.edu/units/music/spec/deedofgift.html.

NOTES

CHAPTER 1

1. A total of 90 out of 123 ARL Libraries (73 percent) responded to this survey. Karlene Noel Jennings and Jos Wanschers, *Library Development*, SPEC Kit 297 (Washington, DC: Association of Research Libraries, 2006), 11.

2. Susannah Cleveland and Mark A. Puente, *MLA Survey of Personnel Characteristics, 2009 Report and Statistical Summary*, http://musiclibraryassoc.org/Publications.aspx?id=798.

3. For the purposes of this discussion, the terms "development" and "fundraising" appear interchangeably in the text. As Kathleen S. Kelly points out, many universities adopted the term "development" in order to counteract possible stigma with the term "fundraising." Kathleen S. Kelly, *Fund Raising and Public Relations: A Critical Analysis* (Hillsdale, NJ: Lawrence Erlbaum Associates, 1991), 7–9.

4. Mark D. Winston and Lisa Dunkley reported in 2002 that only 33.3 percent of ALA-accredited library and information science programs offered marketing courses with fundraising as a component. Mark D. Winston and Lisa Dunkley, "Leadership Competencies for Academic Librarians: The Importance of Development and Fund-raising," *College & Research Libraries* 63 (March 2002): 173. Additional research reveals several new subjects that are being taught in the library science curriculum, but fundraising is usually not mentioned as one of them. See Karen Markey, "Current Educational Trends in the Information and Library Science Curriculum," *Journal of Education for Library and Information Science* 45, no. 4 (Fall 2004): 317–339; and Russell A. Hall, "Exploring the Core: An Examination of Required Courses in ALA-accredited," *Education for Information* 27 Issue 1 (2009): 57–67.

5. In surveying the scholarly literature, Ashlie Keylon Conway found no publications on fundraising for music special collections, and not much other literature that covers fundraising for music libraries in general. Ashlie Keylon Conway, "The Music Librarian as Development Officer: Raising Funds for Special Collections," *Music Reference Services Quarterly* 11, 3/4 (2008): 206–15.

6. For helpful internet resources that cover library fundraising, see Janet L. Balas, "Looking for Funds in All the Right Places," *Computers in Libraries* 26 (September 2006): 23–25: and Nancy K. Herther, "21st-Century Fundraising: Everything You Need May Be Free on the Web," *Searcher* 17 no. 8 (September 2009): 24–31.

7. This discourse does not attempt to survey the current fundraising activities in music libraries nationally; most information is based on the author's personal experience in development work at academic music libraries along with research in current fundraising and library literature. Because of the author's association with the Massachusetts Institute of Technology (MIT), he often describes library situations at MIT in order to cite actual experiences. A sense of fundraising activities at other music libraries was obtained informally through a posting on the Music Library Association's e-mail distribution list (MLA-L) by the author on January 29, 2008. Libraries answered questions about various topics: library newsletters, "donation" links on library homepages, library benefit concerts, and book sales. Music libraries from the following institutions generously responded to this posting: Appalachian State University, Brown University, Carnegie Library of Pittsburgh, Connecticut College, Curtis Institute of Music, Longy School

of Music, Oberlin College, Peabody Institute, University of Hartford, University of South Carolina, University of Washington, and Western Washington University.

8. Herbert S. White, "Seeking Outside Funding: The Right and Wrong Reasons," *Library Journal* 117, no. 12 (July 1, 1992): 48.

9. Karlene Noel Jennings, "Development is Dysfunctional . . . ," *The Bottom Line: Managing Library Finances* 19, no. 4 (2006): 187.

10. A practical, hands-on fundraising guidebook written specifically for the library director is Kimberly A. Thompson and Karlene Noel Jennings, *More Than a Thank You Note: Academic Library Fundraising for the Dean or Director* (Oxford: Chandos Publishing, 2009).

11. Samuel T. Huang, "Where There's a Will, There's a Way: Fundraising for the Academic Library," *The Bottom Line: Managing Library Finances* 19, no. 3 (2006): 147.

12. Adriana Ercolano, " 'But It's Not My Job . . .' The Role Librarians Play in Library Development," *The Bottom Line: Managing Library Finances* 20, no. 2 (2007): 94–96.

13. In a 2006 survey of ARL libraries, 18 percent of library development officers reported having a library science degree. Jennings and Wanschers, *Library Development*, 13.

14. CFRE (Certified Fund Raising Executive) website, http://www.cfre.org.

15. Dana C. Rooks, "Fund Raising: Random Ramblings. Seek Professional Help," *Journal of Academic Librarianship* 33, no. 2 (March 2007): 292.

16. Victoria Steele, "The Role of Special Collections in Library Development," in *Library Fundraising: Models for Success*, ed. Dwight F. Burlingame (Chicago: American Library Association, 1995), 73.

17. Marie A. Kascus, "Fundraising for Smaller Academic Libraries: Strategies for Success," *College & Undergraduate Libraries* 10, no. 1 (2003): 4.

18. Sue Fontaine, "The Role of Public Relations in Fund Raising," *Journal of Library Administration* 12, no. 4 (1990): 15.

19. Many books and articles cover the topic of library promotion and marketing. Several publications in this area appear in Daria Decooman, "Marketing Library Resources: An Annotated Bibliography," *Library Connect*, pamphlet no. 8 (2005): 1–20, http://www.elsevier.com/framework_librarians/LibraryConnect/LCP08 /LCP08.pdf.

20. Kelly, *Fund Raising*, 329–54.

CHAPTER 2

1. *Annual Register of Grant Support 2012: A Directory of Funding Sources*, 45th ed. (Medford, NJ: Information Today, 2011), ix.

2. The process of creating a donor list for a university library—in this case, at Syracuse University—appears in Gregory J. Griffin, "Who's Your Donor? A Practical Approach to Building a Revenue-Producing Library Prospect Database," *The Bottom Line: Managing Library Finances* 18, no. 3 (2005): 138–45.

3. Joe Clark, "Creative Fundraising through Campus Collaborations," *Journal of Library Innovation* 2, no. 2 (September 2011): 65.

4. Stuart M. Basefsky, "Pooled Endowments: A New Funding Idea," *College & Research Libraries News* 56, no. 6 (June 1995): 406.

5. Catherine Quinlan, "The Library's Role in the Capital Campaign: Building a Donor Base for the Library," in *Successful Fundraising: Case Studies of Academic Libraries*, ed. Meredith A. Butler (Washington, DC: Association of Research Libraries, 2001), 96.

6. Brett Bonfield, "What Your Donors (and Would-Be Donors) Wish You Knew," *In the Library with the Lead Pipe* (blog), May 12, 2010, http://www.inthelibrarywiththeleadpipe.org/2010/what-your-donors-and-would-be-donors-wish-you-knew.

7. The Association of Fundraising Professionals (AFP) features an online "Survival Kit for Fundraising in Challenging Times" (updated May 25, 2011, http://www.afpnet.org/ResourceCenter/ArticleDetail.cfm?ItemNumber=3942), which includes over fifty resources that provide advice to fundraisers during an economic downturn. Access to this kit is restricted to AFP members, although a few sample articles are available to nonmembers.

8. Lisa Browar and Samuel A. Streit, "Mutually Assured Survival: Library Fund-Raising Strategies in a Changing Economy," *Library Trends* 52, no. 1 (Summer 2003): 74–75.

9. Cecilia Hogan, "Philanthropy—Not Just for Rock Stars: 'Real People' and Digital Donations," *Searcher: The Magazine for Database Professionals* 15, no. 2 (February 2007): 14.

10. Stanley E. Gornish, "How to Apply Fund-Raising Principles in a Competitive Environment," *Library Administration & Management* 12, no. 2 (Spring 1998): 95.

11. Some of these generational differences, with regard to philanthropy, appear in Betty J. Glass and Vicki L. Toy Smith, "Fundraising and Public Relations in an Electronic Environment," in *Attracting, Educating, and Serving Remote Users through the Web: A How-to-Do-It Manual for Librarians*, ed. Donnelyn Curtis (New York: Neal-Schuman Publishers, 2002), 232–33.

12. Teri M. Vogel and Doug Goans, "Delivering the News with Blogs: The Georgia State University Library Experience," *Internet Reference Services Quarterly* 10, no. 1 (2005): 5–27.

13. Betty K. Bryce notes four kinds of library newsletters: (1) internal use for library employees, (2) external use for campus or community, (3) a fundraising vehicle, and (4) an electronic version available to anyone. Betty K. Bryce, "Using Newsletters in the Library's Communication Strategy," *Library Administration & Management* 10, no. 4 (Fall 1996): 246.

14. Anthony J. Frisby, Daniel G. Kipnis, and Elizabeth G. Mikita, "Developing and Sustaining a Web-Based Library Newsletter," *Medical Reference Services Quarterly* 25, no. 1 (Spring 2006): 18.

15. Bernadette Lopez-Fitzsimmons and Nicholas Taylor, "Online Newsletters in Academic Libraries," *Catholic Library World* 76, no. 1 (September 2005): 44–45.

16. Ibid., 46.

17. The University of Mississippi took a compromise position on the print versus online newsletter question by emailing PDFs of its library faculty newsletters to the English and Theatre Arts departments in 2009 as well as the Journalism department in 2010. The PDF format allowed users to easily print out the newsletter, which would likely appease some faculty members who had indicated a preference for print materials over ebooks and online journals. However, a 2010 survey of this newsletter service surprisingly revealed that 68% of the survey participants read the newsletter on a Web browser, while none of the survey participants printed the newsletter out. For more details, see Alex Watson, "Library Newsletters in Print and Digital Formats: Faculty Preferences in a Hybrid Format," *Internet Reference Services Quarterly* 16 Issue 4 (2011): 199–210.

18. Kim Klein, *Fundraising for Social Change* (San Francisco: Jossey-Bass, 2007), 204.

19. Dan Zager, "From the Librarian," *The Sibley Muse: Newsletter of the Sibley Music Library*, 27, no. 3 (May 2008): 2–3, http://www.esm.rochester.edu/sibley/muse/SibleyMuse27.3.pdf.

20. Western Washington University Music Library, Friends of the Music Library, *High Notes*, http://library.wwu.edu/page/4540.

21. Marian Ritter, e-mail message to author, August 5, 2008.

22. Marian Ritter, "The Friends of the Music Library at Western Washington University," *Music Reference Services Quarterly* 9, no. 2 (2005): 59.

23. Ibid.

24. Massachusetts Institute of Technology, Lewis Music Library, *What's the Score?*, http://libraries.mit.edu/music/news/news-index.html.

25. For more details about this newsletter, see Christie Moore and Peter Munstedt, "Brother, Can You Spare a Few Thousand? Raising Money with a Library Newsletter," poster session presented at the Music Library Association meeting, Chicago, February 20, 2009, http://musiclibraryassoc2009postersessions.blogspot.com/2009/04/brother-can-you-spare-few-thousand.html. See also appendix 1, Library Newsletter.

26. Paul A. Willis and Paula L. Pope, "Building Endowment through a Major Gifts Program," in *Successful Fundraising: Case Studies of Academic Libraries*, ed. Meredith A. Butler (Washington, D.C.: Association of Research Libraries, 2001), 67.

27. For examples of various topics in university fundraising flash presentations, see the following websites: University of Waterloo, "Library Campaign," December 15, 2005, http://www.lib.uwaterloo.ca/develop/kresge_flash; George Mason University, Office of Annual Giving, [General university appeal], http://www.gmu.edu/development/annual/studentpromo.html; Massachusetts Institute of Technology, Sloan School of Management, "The MIT Sloan Experience," http://mitsloan.mit.edu/E&I-reunion2007.

28. Increasing numbers of music libraries are using YouTube to promote their services. An overview of this participation is presented in: Nick Homenda, "Music Libraries on YouTube," *Music Reference Services Quarterly* 14, issue 1–2 (2011): 30–45. Music library tours, promotions, and interviews with library staff are typical presentations. Early examples of music libraries appearing on YouTube include: a library tour in "Tour the Music Library at the University of Florida," May 5, 2008, http://www.youtube.com/watch?v=RhzgYIRjwr4; and a request by the University of South Carolina music library staff asking users to recommend new materials for its collection: "USC Music Library Blog, Episode 1: Hit Us Up," September 20, 2007, http://www.youtube.com/watch?v=YHPeZS4g-QU. An early illustration of a music library podcast includes an interview with Tufts University music librarian Michael Rogan discussing the new music library: "Tisch Talks: The Tisch Library Podcast Series, Episode Four: The Lilly Music Library," April 23, 2007, http://www.library.tufts.edu/tisch/tischTalks.html.

29. From the author's informal observation, the number of academic music libraries with a Facebook presence seemed to remain relatively small until around the year 2009, when increasing numbers of music libraries established Facebook pages.

30. Issues involved with MySpace and Facebook for academic libraries appear in Melanie Chu and Yvonne Nalani Meulemans, "The Problems and Potential of MySpace and Facebook Usage in Academic Libraries," *Internet Reference Services Quarterly* 13, no. 1 (2008): 69–85; and Laurie Charnigo and Paula Barnett-Ellis, "Checking Out Facebook.com: The Impact of a Digital Trend on Academic Libraries," *Information Technology and Libraries* (March 2007): 23–34.

31. Facebook, "Causes" (application), http://apps.facebook.com/causes.

32. For more information on fundraising through social networking, see Ted Hart, James M. Greenfield, and Sheeraz D. Haji, *People to People Fundraising: Social Networking and Web 2.0 for Charities* (Hoboken, NJ: John Wiley & Sons, 2007).

33. The definition of "major giving" varies from university to university. In 2000, Steele and Elder wrote that small libraries may think of $10,000 as a major gift, while larger libraries would regard a donation starting at $100,000 to be in that category. The authors also indicate that many fundraisers consider $25,000 to be the minimum amount for a major gift. Victoria Steele and Stephen D. Elder, *Becoming a Fundraiser: The Principles and Practice of Library Development* (Chicago: American Library Association, 2000), 25.

34. For more details on case statements, see Stanley E. Gornish, "How to Apply Fund-Raising Principles in a Competitive Environment," *Library Administration & Management* 12, no. 2 (Spring 1998): 100.

35. Not all fundraisers endorse case statements. Victoria Steele and Stephen D. Elder make several arguments against their usefulness. Steele and Elder, *Becoming a Fundraiser*, 57.

36. Details about passive fundraising appear in James Swan, *Fundraising for Libraries: 25 Proven Ways to Get More Money for Your Library* (New York: Neal-Schuman Publishers, 2002), 113–24.

37. Matthew Simon, "Fundraising as a Small Business Enterprise," *The Bottom Line: Managing Library Finances* 10, no. 2 (1997): 107.

38. Several publications discussed libraries' internet fundraising when this topic was new. Examples include Adam Corson-Finnerty and Laura Blanchard, *Fundraising and Friend-Raising on the Web* (Chicago: American Library Association, 1998); Donnelyn Curtis, ed., *Attracting, Educating, and Serving Remote Users through the Web: A How-to-Do-It Manual for Librarians* (New York: Neal-Schuman Publishers, 2002); and David King, "Soliciting Virtual Money," *Library Journal, Net Connect* 125, 14 (Fall 2000): 39–41.

39. A survey of 106 academic libraries conducted from December 2003 through February 2004 indicates that just 28.2 percent of library homepages include a direct link for donations or gifts. Jeanie M. Welch, "The Electronic Welcome Mat: The Academic Library Web Site as a Marketing and Public Relations Tool," *Journal of Academic Librarianship* 31, no. 3 (May 2005): 227. In an Association of Research Libraries survey of ARL member libraries from March 2006, however, 90 percent of responding institutions report that a library donation option is present on their university's giving web page. Jennings and Wanschers, *Library Development*, 15.

40. Glen E. Holt and George Horn, "Taking Donations in Cyberspace," *The Bottom Line: Managing Library Finances* 18, no. 1 (2005): 26.

41. Adam Corson-Finnerty, "Cybergifts," *Library Trends* 48, no. 3 (Winter 2000): 624–28.

42. Klein, *Fundraising for Social Change*, 179. For more details about the telephone as a development tool, see the chapter "Fundraising by Telephone," pp. 179–98.

43. Karen Horny, "An Unexpected Fundraising Success," *Library Leadership & Management* 23, no. 3 (Summer 2009): 131–32, 149.

44. Judy Tsou, e-mail message to author, January 29, 2008.

45. "In Europe, a Library Erotica Hotline," *Library Journal* (June 1, 2007): 13.

46. To learn how the library at George Mason University involved alumni nondonors in its annual giving program, see Adriana Ercolano, "Remember the Annual Fund! Small Steps to Build and Sustain a Library Annual Giving Alumni Program," *The Bottom Line: Managing Library Finances* 20, no. 1 (2007): 50–53.

47. Emily Silverman, "Beyond Luck and Money, Building Your Base: Identifying Library Donors," *The Bottom Line: Managing Library Finances* 21, no. 4 (2008): 140.

48. For discussions concerning partnerships between sports and libraries, see Jennifer Paustenbaugh and Lynn Trojahn, "Annual Fund Programs for Academic Libraries," *Library Trends* 48, no. 3 (Winter 2000): 579–96; and James G. Neal, "College Sports and Library Fundraising," *The Bottom Line: Managing Library Finances* 10, no. 2 (1997): 58–59.

49. A capital campaign commonly refers to a fundraising drive that supports all kinds of projects. The present discussion uses that broad definition of the term. The terminology that describes capital campaigns, however, varies within the development field. Some development people refer to a comprehensive campaign in an all-inclusive sense while referring to a capital campaign as a narrower subset that supports just buildings and building projects. See Thompson and Jennings, *More Than a Thank You Note*, 77.

50. For those librarians who must do the asking themselves and need advice on overcoming any trepidations, see Laura Fredricks, *The Ask: How to Ask Anyone for Any Amount for Any Purpose* (San Francisco: Jossey-Bass, 2006).

51. Andrea R. Lapsley, "Donor Acknowledgement and Recognition: A Not So Simple Thank You," *The Bottom Line: Managing Library Finances* 10, no. 4 (1997): 190.

52. Mal Warwick, *How to Write Successful Fundraising Letters* (San Francisco: Jossey-Bass, 2008), 93. This book even includes a section entitled "Ninety Ways to Use the Word 'You' in a Fundraising Letter," 273–75.

53. Ibid, 214, 217.

54. Public charities can be ruthless in their pursuit of donations. As an experiment, a woman sent small checks of $20 to $25 to thirty-eight charities in 2010. In response to her gifts, she received 678 letters from 164 charities. One organization sent her 24 letters within the year. Daniel Rubin, "Keeping Count of Charity Mail: Deluged by Solicitations, She Devised an Experiment," *Philadelphia Inquirer*, February 10, 2011, B1, B6.

55. Lapsley, "Donor Acknowledgement and Recognition," 188–90.

56. Klein, *Fundraising for Social Change*, 232.

57. Lapsley, "Donor Acknowledgement and Recognition," 188.

58. Klein, *Fundraising for Social Change*, 232.

59. Anne Ruggiero and Julia Zimmerman, "Grateful Recipients: Library Staff as Active Participants in Fund-Raising," *Library Administration & Management* 18, no. 3 (Summer 2004): 142.

60. Johanna Olson Alexander, "Fundraising for the Evolving Academic Library: The Strategic Small Shop Advantage," *Journal of Academic Librarianship* 24, no. 2 (March 1998): 134.

61. For the background behind one such artist-designed bookplate, see Jeffrey Garrett, "Northwestern's New Maeda Bookplate: Capturing Continuity and Change in an Image for the 21st Century," *College & Research Libraries News* 65, no. 7 (July/August 2004): 376–78.

CHAPTER 3

1. The acquisition of gifts in kind at a major research music library is documented by Hugh Cobbe, who describes his experience working in the British Library. See Hugh Cobbe, "Gifts, Purchases, the Lottery and the Treasury: Some Personal Reflections on 25 Years of Music Acquisitions at the British Library," *Fontes Artis Musicae* 48, no. 3 (July–September 2001): 237–45.

2. Practical suggestions for assessing donations of music materials are summarized in: Elizabeth Nichol, "Out of the Boxes. Treasures from the Donations Pile – Some Hints for Assessment. Notes from

an Interactive Session at the IAML(NZ) Conference, Auckland, November 2008, Led by Cathy Williams and Roger Flury of the National Library of New Zealand," *Crescendo: Bulletin of the International Association of Music Libraries* 81 (December 2008): 19–20.

3. John Ballestro and Philip C. Howze, "When a Gift is Not a Gift: Collection Assessment Using Cost-Benefit Analysis," *Collection Management* 30, no. 3 (2005): 49–66.

4. For details concerning components of a contract, see Tinker Massey, "Management of Gift Materials in an Academic Library," *Collection Building* 24, no. 3 (2005): 80. For a concise description of deeds of gift, see: The Society of American Archivists, "A Guide to Deeds of Gift," www.archivists.org/publications/deed_of_gift.asp. Examples of gift information that selected music library websites provide to potential donors appear in appendix 2.

5. Benita Strnad, "How to Look a Gift Horse in the Mouth, or, How to Tell People You Can't Use Their Old Junk in Your Library," *Collection Building* 14, no. 2 (1995): 30.

6. Kristin Heath and Terra Merkey, "Gifts 101: A Systematic Approach for Gifts of Music," *Music Reference Services Quarterly* 14, issue 4 (2011): 183–202.

7. To establish the monetary value of gifts in kind, see Department of the Treasury, Internal Revenue Service, Publication 561, "Determining the Value of Donated Property," rev. April 2007, http://www.irs.gov/pub/irs-pdf/p561.pdf.

8. Department of the Treasury, Internal Revenue Service, Publication 526, "Charitable Contributions: For Use in Preparing 2010 Returns," 19, http://www.irs.gov/pub/irs-pdf/p526.pdf.

9. Department of the Treasury, Internal Revenue Service, "Instructions for Form 8283: Noncash Charitable Contributions," rev. December 2006, 1–2, http://www.irs.gov/pub/irs-pdf/i8283.pdf.

10. Ibid., 6–7.

11. John Lubrano, co-owner of J & J Lubrano Music Antiquarians, notes that the kind of appraiser one employs depends upon the type of music donated. He suggests for rare collectible items to check with the Antiquarian Booksellers' Association of America at http://www.abaa.org/books/abaa; for autograph manuscripts, look for appraisers in the Professional Autograph Dealers Association at http://www.padaweb.org; and for noncollectible music, contact music dealers or music professionals who know the music trade. John Lubrano, comment on the Music Library Association Mailing List (MLA-L), April 7, 2008, https://listserv.indiana.edu/cgi-bin/wa-iub.exe?A2=MLA-L;MvC6fg;20080407125604-0400A. In addition, the IRS provides detailed advice on appraisals and appraisers in Department of the Treasury, Publication 561, 8–11. Music librarians might also want to keep their own lists of qualified local and national appraisers. See the American Society of Appraisers website at http://www.appraisers.org/FindanAppraiser/FindAnAppraiser.aspx.

12. For laws concerning charitable contributions, see Department of the Treasury, Internal Revenue Service, Publication 526.

13. Joan M. Hood, "Fundraising for Libraries: Four Important Elements," *Library Issues* 13, no. 6 (1993): 2.

14. John McKee, "What Every Library Can (and Should) Do to Increase Private Support through Planned Gifts," *The Bottom Line: Managing Library Finances* 16, no. 4 (2003): 151–52.

15. Browar and Streit, "Mutually Assured Survival," 82.

16. Steele and Elder, *Becoming a Fundraiser*, 110.

17. Some resources that describe planned giving possibilities include Richard D. Barrett and Molly E. Ware, *Planned Giving Essentials: A Step by Step Guide to Success* (Gaithersburg, MD: Aspen

Publishers, 1997), 35–58; James M. Hodge and David B. Richardson, "The Role of Planned Giving," *Journal of Library Administration* 12, no. 4 (1990): 121–34; Amy Sherman Smith and Matthew D. Lehrer, *Legacies for Libraries: A Practical Guide to Planned Giving* (Chicago: American Library Association, 2000), 38–73. Also explore the "Giving" pages, found on many university library web sites, which often explain planned giving options in a clear, succinct manner that potential donors can understand.

18. Basefsky, "Pooled Endowments," 406.

19. Robert C. Miller, "Endowment Funding in Academic Libraries: Pitfalls and Potential," *The Bottom Line* 1, no. 1 (1987): 24.

20. For example, a disgruntled donor to athletic facilities at the University of Connecticut requested his three million dollars back because of disagreements—including the choice of a new football coach—with the school's athletic director. Mike DiMauro, "Major UConn Donor Demands Return of $3 Million," *The Day*, January 26, 2011, http://www.theday.com/article/20110126/SPORT07/301259947.

21. To learn about Cornell University's work to establish a pooled endowment for research periodicals, see Basefsky, "Pooled Endowments," 406.

22. Miller, "Endowment Funding," 25.

23. Harvard University, Loeb Music Library, "History," http://hcl.harvard.edu/libraries/loebmusic/history.html.

CHAPTER 4

1. For descriptions of special library events and advice on how to run them, see April L. Harris, "Special Events and their Role in Fund Raising," *Journal of Library Administration* 12, no. 4 (1990): 39–51.

2. Michael Page Miller, a lead faculty member for the Fund Raising School and a partner in Miller Rollins (New York), presents several reasons why organizations should reconsider holding special events to raise money. Michael Page Miller, "Nine and a Half Theses about Fundraising Benefits: Rationalizations, Indulgences, and Opportunity Costs," in *Alternative Revenue Sources: Prospects, Requirements, and Concerns for Nonprofits*, ed. Dwight F. Burlingame and Warren F. Ilchman (San Francisco: Jossey-Bass, 1996), 109–17.

3. Leonard Lehrman, "Hear the Music: Concerts in Libraries," *Wilson Library Bulletin* 69 (February 1995): 30–32.

4. To learn about methods of organizing mostly large-scale music concerts, see James F. Hollan, *The Concert Book* (Chicago: Bonus Books, 1999).

5. A library benefit performance by comedian Bill Cosby in 1998, for example, raised $125,000 for the Lenox (MA) Library Association's capital campaign. "Money Matters: Network, Network, Network," *American Libraries* 29, no. 7 (August 1998): 37.

6. The Newberry Consort website provides the following information about the Newberry Consort and its relationship to the Newberry Library: ". . . the ensemble plumbs the Newberry Library's vast music collection and assembles a star-studded roster of local and international artists to bring you world-class performances of music from the 13th to the 18th centuries . . . and occasionally beyond! Affiliated with the Newberry Library Center for Renaissance Studies, the Consort also serves as an ensemble-in-residence at both the University of Chicago and Northwestern University." The Newberry Consort, "About Us," http://www.newberryconsort.org/about.

7. "The public attention, which has brought to her as an artist, is for Anne-Sophie Mutter also an obligation to point to and to alleviate the medical and social problems of our times—and to give regular

benefit concerts to this end." Anne-Sophie Mutter web page, "Charity Engagement," http://www.anne-sophie-mutter.de/benefizkonzerte-karitativ.html?&L=1. Among the performances listed on this website is a library benefit concert on October 17, 2003, in Berlin to benefit the Anna Amalia Library in Weimar.

8. Peter A. Munstedt, "Library Benefit Concerts: Blood, Sweat, and Cash," *College & Research Libraries News* 50, no. 3 (March 1989): 205–8.

9. Each library will need to determine its own set of circumstances regarding licensing fees for music performed at benefit concerts. The American Library Association retained a law firm to address the issue of licensing laws for music performed in libraries. For these guidelines, see Robert A. Wynbrandt, "Musical Performances in Libraries: Is a License from ASCAP Required?" *Public Libraries* 29 (July/August 1990): 224–25.

10. Department of the Treasury, Publication 526, 3–4.

11. To learn about components of staffing for various types of book sales, see Audrey Fenner, "Library Book Sales: A Cost-Benefit Analysis," *Library Collections, Acquisitions, & Technical Services* 29, no. 2 (2005): 154, 156, 159.

12. Ibid., 166–67.

13. Kathy Wachel, "Management of Gifts to Libraries, Part IV, Selling Gifts-in-Kind on Consignment: The University of Iowa Libraries Model," *Against the Grain* 14, no. 6 (December 2002/January 2003): 92.

14. Pat Ditzler and JoAnn Dumas, "Inside Pandora's Box: Anatomy of a Used Book Sale," *Against the Grain* 13, no. 3 (June 2001): 89–90.

15. For a list of appraisers, online booksellers, and auction websites, see Cecilia Hogan, "Library Book Sales," *Searcher* 16, no. 3 (March 2008): 36–46.

16. Bob Kackley et al., "From Clutter to Cash: Online Book Sales at the University of Maryland's Engineering and Physical Sciences Library (EPSL)," *Collection Management* 31, no. 3 (2006): 83.

17. Stephanie Gerding and Mary Billings, "Online Book Sales for Libraries: Turning Discards and Donations into Cash," *Public Libraries* 46, no. 1 (January/February 2007): 33, 35.

18. Ibid, 35.

19. "Our Impact," Better World Books website, http://www.betterworldbooks.com/info.aspx?f=our_impact.

20. For fuller details concerning fundraising techniques on eBay, see Greg Holden and Jill Finlayson, *Fundraising on eBay: How to Raise Big Money on the World's Greatest Online Marketplace* (New York: McGraw-Hill, 2005).

21. The University of Hawaii at Manoa and Western Oregon University obtained library materials through online auctions. To learn about the experiences of these two libraries, see Amy J. Carlson, "You Are the Top Bidder! Beginning the Online Auction Process," in *Charleston Conference Proceedings 2005*, ed. Beth R. Bernhardt, Tim Daniels, and Kim Steinle (Westport, Connecticut: Libraries Unlimited, 2006), 145–50; and Camila Gabaldón, "Building Library Collections, the eBay Way," *Electronic Journal of Academic and Special Librarianship* 6, no. 3 (Winter 2005), http://southernlibrarianship.icaap.org/content/v06n03/gabaldon_c01.htm.

22. For examples of public libraries selling unwanted materials through the internet, see Kathleen Baxter, "Your Discards May Be Somebody's Treasure," *Library Journal* 125, no. 6 (April 1, 2000): 62–63; Dale S. Hill, "Selling Withdrawn and Gift Books on eBay: Does it Make Sense?," *Journal of Interlibrary Loan, Document Delivery & Information Supply* 14, no. 2 (2003): 37–40; and Peter Schworm, "Public

Libraries Use Internet to Sell Old Books, Help Budgets," *TechNewsWorld* (December 1, 2003): 1–3, http://www.abebooks.com/docs/CompanyInformation/PressRoom/techNewsWorldDec12003.pdf. To understand how a university archive successfully sells items on eBay, see Michael Doylen, "Experiments in Deaccessioning: Archives and On-Line Auctions," *American Archivist* 64 (Fall/Winter 2001): 350–62. All of the above articles report positive results in selling library items through online auctions.

23. Lisa A. Beinhoff, "How Online Auctions Threaten Library Collections," *American Libraries* 31, no. 3 (March 2000): 53–54.

24. The name failed to sell on eBay for the original $375,000 reserve price in an auction that ended on February 9, 2006. A second eBay auction, posted from February 14–24, 2006, lowered the starting bid to $300,000 with no reserve. No bids were received in the latter auction. "On eBay, Hoping for a Donor," *Library Journal* 131, no. 5 (March 15, 2006): 13.

25. Marjorie Hassen, "An Overview of the IAML-U.S. Donated Music Materials Program," *Fontes Artis Musicae* 53, Issue 1 (January–March 2006): 20.

26. Music Library Association, "Donated Music Materials Program," http://www.musiclibraryassoc.org/awards.aspx?id=1001.

27. Ibid.

28. American Library Association, "Sending Books to Needy Libraries: Book Donation Programs," ALA Fact Sheet 12, last modified May 2011, http://www.ala.org/ala/professionalresources/libfactsheets/alalibraryfactsheet12.cfm.

29. Sally Gardner Reed, Beth Nawalinski, and Alexander Peterson. *101+ Great Ideas for Libraries and Friends: Marketing, Fundraising, Friends Development, and More!* (New York: Neal-Schuman Publishers, 2004), 29–30.

30. Marian Ritter, "The Friends of the Music Library," 55–60.

31. Carnegie Library of Pittsburgh, "Friends of the Music Library," http://www.clpgh.org/research/music/aboutcollection.html#friends.

32. Thompson and Jennings, *More Than a Thank You Note*, 52.

33. For a discussion of the pros and cons of library friends groups, see Frank D'Andraia, Jessica Fitzpatrick, and Catherine Oliver, "Academic Libraries and Friends Groups: Asset or Liability?," *Journal of Library Administration* 51 (2011): 221–30.

CHAPTER 5

1. Some examples of guides to writing successful library grants include Cynthia Anderson and Kathi Knop, *Write Grants, Get Money* (Columbus, OH: Linworth Books, 2009); Peggy Barber and Linda D. Crowe, *Getting Your Grant: A How-to-Do-It Manual for Librarians*; Herbert B. Landau, *Winning Library Grants: A Game Plan* (Chicago: American Library Association, 2011); and Pamela H. MacKellar and Stephanie K. Gerding, *Winning Grants: A How-to-Do-It Manual for Librarians with Multimedia Tutorials and Grant Development Tools* (New York: Neal-Schuman Publishers, 2010).

2. *Annual Register of Grant Support 2012: A Directory of Funding Sources*, 45th ed. (Medford, NJ: Information Today, 2011), ix.

3. For details on interpreting this form, see Peter Swords, "How to Read the IRS Form 990," Nonprofit Coordinating Committee of New York website, (free registration required), http://www.npccny.org/new990/new990.htm.

4. Much of the information describing foundations is obtained from *The Foundation Directory 2011*, 33rd ed. (New York: Foundation Center, 2011), vi; and Barber and Crowe, *Getting Your Grant*, 65–66.

5. Barber Crowe, *Getting your Grant*, 65.

6. For a list of local community foundations, see "Community Foundations," Council on Foundations website, http://www.cof.org/whoweserve/community/resources/index.cfm?navItemNumber=15626#locator.

7. Andrew W. Mellon Foundation, "Scholarly Communications and Information Technology: Overview," http://www.mellon.org/grant_programs/programs/scholarlycommunications#overview.

8. Andrew W. Mellon Foundation, "Report from January 1, 2010 through December 31, 2010," 66–77. http://www.mellon.org/news_publications/annual-reports-essays/annual-reports/content2010.pdf.

9. To find these Foundation Center locations, see "Find Us," Grant Space website, http://grantspace.org/Find-Us.

10. Herther, "21st-Century Fundraising," 25.

11. "About Us," Institute of Museum and Library Services website, http://www.imls.gov/about.

12. "Recent Grant Awards," National Endowment for the Humanities website, http://www.neh.gov/news/recentawards.html.

13. For instance, the Michigan State University Libraries website offers a detailed listing of fundraising resources: "Grants for Nonprofits: Libraries," http://staff.lib.msu.edu/harris23/grants/2lib.htm.

14. "Council for the Arts at MIT (CAMIT)," website, http://arts.mit.edu/about/council.

15. "Program for the Preservation of Classical Music Historical Recordings," Association for Recorded Sound Collections website, http://www.arsc-audio.org/preservationgrants.html.

CHAPTER 6

1. Tinker Massey, "Management of Gift Materials in an Academic Library," 82.

2. Ruggiero and Zimmerman, "Grateful Recipients," 141.

3. Association of Fundraising Professionals, Association of Healthcare Philanthropy, Council for Advancement and Support of Education, and the Giving Institute, "Donor Bill of Rights," http://www.afpnet.org/Ethics/EnforcementDetail.cfm?ItemNumber=3359.

4. The two philanthropic organizations that attract the membership of many university library development officers are the Association for Fundraising Professionals (AFP) and the Council for Advancement and Support of Education (CASE). Each organization has its own set of ethical standards. AFP's "Code of Ethical Principles and Standards" was adopted in 1964 and amended in 2007 (see http://www.afpnet.org/Ethics/EnforcementDetail.cfm?ItemNumber=3261). CASE has several statements concerning ethics. Its general statement is the "CASE Statement of Ethics," adopted in 1982 (see http://www.case.org/Samples_Research_and_Tools/Ethics_Resources_and_Issues/CASE_Statement_of_Ethics.html). Additional CASE statements cover various aspects of development.

5. "Code of Ethics of the American Library Association," American Library Association website, http://www.ala.org/ala/issuesadvocacy/proethics/codeofethics/codeethics.cfm. The code was adopted in 1939 by the ALA Council and amended June 30, 1981, June 28, 1995, and January 22, 2008.

6. Marilyn Fischer, *Ethical Decision Making in Fund Raising* (New York: John Wiley & Sons, 2000), 20–31.

7. Some libraries will offer enticements to elicit donations. For example, the Queens College Libraries, including the Music Library, offer one-year circulation privileges for a donation of $50 or more (see appendix 2).

8. Kelly, *Fund Raising*, 219.

BIBLIOGRAPHY

BOOKS AND ARTICLES

Alexander, Johanna Olson. "Fundraising for the Evolving Academic Library: The Strategic Small Shop Advantage." *Journal of Academic Librarianship* 24, no. 2 (March 1998): 131–38.

Anderson, Cynthia, and Kathi Knop. *Write Grants, Get Money.* Columbus, Ohio: Linworth Books, 2009.

Annual Register of Grant Support 2012: A Directory of Funding Sources. 45th ed. Medford, NJ: Information Today, 2011.

Balas, Janet L. "Looking for Funds in All the Right Places." *Computers in Libraries* 26 (September 2006): 23–25.

Ballestro, John, and Philip C. Howze. "When a Gift is Not a Gift: Collection Assessment Using Cost-Benefit Analysis." *Collection Management* 30, no. 3 (2005): 49–66.

Barber, Peggy, and Linda D. Crowe. *Getting Your Grant: A How-to-Do-It Manual for Librarians.* New York: Neal-Schuman Publishers, 1993.

Barrett, Richard D., and Molly E. Ware. *Planned Giving Essentials: A Step by Step Guide to Success.* Gaithersburg, MD: Aspen Publishers, 1997.

Basefsky, Stuart M. "Pooled Endowments: A New Funding Idea." *College & Research Libraries News* 56, no. 6 (June 1995): 405–7.

Baxter, Kathleen. "Your Discards May Be Somebody's Treasure." *Library Journal* 125, no. 6 (April 1, 2000): 62–63.

Beinhoff, Lisa A. "How Online Auctions Threaten Library Collections." *American Libraries* 31, no. 3 (March 2000): 53–54.

Bonfield, Brett. "What Your Donors (and Would-Be Donors) Wish You Knew." *In the Library with the Lead Pipe* (blog). May 12, 2010. http://www.inthelibrarywiththeleadpipe.org/2010/what-your-donors-and-would-be-donors-wish-you-knew.

Browar, Lisa, and Samuel A. Streit. "Mutually Assured Survival: Library Fund-Raising Strategies in a Changing Economy." *Library Trends* 52, no. 1 (Summer 2003): 69–86.

Bryce, Betty. K. "Using Newsletters in the Library's Communication Strategy." *Library Administration & Management* 10, no. 4 (Fall 1996): 246–51.

Carlson, Amy J. "You are the Top Bidder! Beginning the Online Auction Process." In *Charleston Conference Proceedings 2005*, edited by Beth R. Bernhardt, Tim Daniels, and Kim Steinle, 145–50. Westport, CT: Libraries Unlimited, 2006.

Charnigo, Laurie, and Paula Barnett-Ellis. "Checking Out Facebook.com: The Impact of a Digital Trend on Academic Libraries." *Information Technology and Libraries* 26, no. 1 (March 2007): 23–34.

Chu, Melanie, and Yvonne Nalani Meulemans. "The Problems and Potential of MySpace and Facebook Usage in Academic Libraries." *Internet Reference Services Quarterly* 13, no. 1 (2008): 69–85.

Clark, Joe. "Creative Fundraising through Campus Collaborations." *Journal of Library Innovation* 2, no. 2 (September 2011): 62–67.

Cleveland, Susannah and Mark A. Puente. *MLA Survey of Personnel Characteristics, 2009 Report and Statistical Summary.* accessed March 4, 2012. http://musiclibraryassoc.org/Publications.aspx?id=798.

Cobbe, Hugh. "Gifts, Purchases, the Lottery and the Treasury: Some Personal Reflections on 25 Years of Music Acquisitions at the British Library." *Fontes Artis Musicae* 48, no. 3 (July–Sept, 2001): 237–45.

Conway, Ashlie Keylon. "The Music Librarian as Development Officer: Raising Funds for Special Collections." *Music Reference Services Quarterly* 11, 3/4 (2008): 203–28.

Corson-Finnerty, Adam. "Cybergifts." *Library Trends* 48, no. 3 (Winter 2000): 619–33.

Corson-Finnerty, Adam, and Laura Blanchard. *Fundraising and Friend-Raising on the Web.* Chicago: American Library Association. 1998.

Curtis, Donnelyn, ed. *Attracting, Educating, and Serving Remote Users through the Web: A How-to-Do-It Manual for Librarians.* New York: Neal-Schuman Publishers, 2002.

D'Andraia, Frank, Jessica Fitzpatrick, and Catherine Oliver. "Academic Libraries and Friends Groups: Asset or Liability?" *Journal of Library Administration* 51 (2011): 221–30.

Decooman, Daria. "Marketing Library Resources: An Annotated Bibliography." *Library Connect*, pamphlet no. 8 (2005): 1–20. http://www.elsevier.com/framework_librarians/LibraryConnect/LCP08/LCP08.pdf.

DiMauro, Mike. "Major UConn Donor Demands Return of $3 Million." *The Day*, January 26, 2011. http://www.theday.com/article/20110126/SPORT07/301259947.

Directory of Music Foundations 2009–2010. Sydney, Australia: Asia Pacific InfoServ Pty Ltd, 2009.

Ditzler, Pat, and JoAnn Dumas. "Inside Pandora's Box: Anatomy of a Used Book Sale." *Against the Grain* 13, no. 3 (June 2001): 89–90.

Doylen, Michael. "Experiments in Deaccessioning: Archives and On-line Auctions." *American Archivist* 64 (Fall/Winter 2001): 350–62.

Ercolano, Adriana. " 'But It's Not My Job . . .': The Role Librarians Play in Library Development." *The Bottom Line: Managing Library Finances* 20, no. 2 (2007): 94–96.

———. "Remember the Annual Fund! Small Steps to Build and Sustain a Library Annual Giving Alumni Program." *The Bottom Line: Managing Library Finances* 20, no. 1 (2007): 50–53.

Fenner, Audrey. "Library Book Sales: A Cost-Benefit Analysis." *Library Collections, Acquisitions, & Technical Services* 29, no. 2 (2005): 149–68.

Fischer, Marilyn. *Ethical Decision Making in Fund Raising.* New York: John Wiley & Sons, 2000.

Fontaine, Sue. "The Role of Public Relations in Fund Raising." *Journal of Library Administration* 12, no. 4 (1990): 15–38.

The Foundation Directory 2011. 33rd ed. New York: Foundation Center, 2011.

Fredricks, Laura. *The Ask: How to Ask Anyone for Any Amount for Any Purpose.* San Francisco: Jossey-Bass, 2006.

Frisby, Anthony J., Daniel G. Kipnis, and Elizabeth G. Mikita. "Developing and Sustaining a Web-Based Library Newsletter." *Medical Reference Services Quarterly* 25, no. 1 (Spring 2006): 17–25.

Gabaldón, Camila. "Building Library Collections, the eBay Way." *Electronic Journal of Academic and Special Librarianship* 6, no. 3 (Winter 2005). http://southernlibrarianship.icaap.org/content/v06n03/gabaldon_c01.htm.

Garrett, Jeffrey. "Northwestern's New Maeda Bookplate: Capturing Continuity and Change in an Image for the 21st Century." *College & Research Libraries News* 65, no. 7 (July/August 2004): 376–78.

Gerding, Stephanie, and Mary Billings. "Online Book Sales for Libraries: Turning Discards and Donations into Cash." *Public Libraries* 46, no. 1 (January/February 2007): 32–35.

Glass, Betty J., and Vicki L. Toy Smith. "Fundraising and Public Relations in an Electronic Environment." In *Attracting, Educating, and Serving Remote Users through the Web: A How-to-Do-It Manual for Librarians*, edited by Donnelyn Curtis, 227–58. New York: Neal-Schuman Publishers, 2002.

Gornish, Stanley E. "How to Apply Fund-Raising Principles in a Competitive Environment." *Library Administration & Management* 12, no. 2 (Spring 1998): 94–103.

Griffin, Gregory J. "Who's Your Donor? A Practical Approach to Building a Revenue-Producing Library Prospect Database." *The Bottom Line: Managing Library Finances* 18, no. 3 (2005): 138–45.

Hall, Russell A. "Exploring the Core: An Examination of Required Courses in ALA-accredited." *Education for Information* 27 Issue 1 (2009): 57-67.

Harris, April L. "Special Events and Their Role in Fund Raising." *Journal of Library Administration* 12, no. 4 (1990): 39–51.

Hart, Ted, James M. Greenfield, and Sheeraz D. Haji. *People to People Fundraising: Social Networking and Web 2.0 for Charities.* Hoboken, NJ: John Wiley & Sons, 2007.

Hassen, Marjorie. "An Overview of the IAML-U.S. Donated Music Materials Program." *Fontes Artis Musicae* 53, Issue 1 (January–March 2006): 17–20.

Heath, Kristin and Terra Merkey. "Gifts 101: A Systematic Approach for Gifts of Music." *Music Reference Services Quarterly* 14, issue 4 (2011): 183–202.

Herther, Nancy K. "21st-Century Fundraising: Everything You Need May Be Free on the Web." *Searcher* 17 no. 8 (September 2009): 24–31.

Hill, Dale S. "Selling Withdrawn and Gift Books on eBay: Does It Make Sense?" *Journal of Interlibrary Loan, Document Delivery & Information Supply* 14, no. 2 (2003): 37–40.

Hodge, James M., and David B. Richardson. "The Role of Planned Giving." *Journal of Library Administration* 12, no. 4 (1990): 121–34.

Hogan, Cecilia. "Library Book Sales." *Searcher* 16, no. 3 (March 2008): 36–46.

———. "Philanthropy—Not Just for Rock Stars: 'Real People' and Digital Donations." *Searcher* 15, no. 2 (February 2007): 13–23.

Holden, Greg, and Jill Finlayson. *Fundraising on eBay: How to Raise Big Money on the World's Greatest Online Marketplace.* New York: McGraw-Hill, 2005.

Hollan, James F. *The Concert Book.* Chicago: Bonus Books, 1999.

Holt, Glen E., and George Horn. "Taking Donations in Cyberspace." *The Bottom Line: Managing Library Finances* 18, no. 1 (2005): 24–28.

Homenda, Nick. "Music Libraries on YouTube." *Music Reference Services Quarterly* 14, issue 1–2 (2011): 30–45.

Hood, Joan M. "Fundraising for Libraries: Four Important Elements." *Library Issues* 13, no. 6 (1993): 1–2.

Horny, Karen. "An Unexpected Fundraising Success." *Library Leadership & Management* 23, no. 3 (Summer 2009): 131–32, 149.

Huang, Samuel T. "Where There's a Will, There's a Way: Fundraising for the Academic Library." *The Bottom Line: Managing Library Finances* 19, no. 3 (2006): 146–51.

"In Europe, a Library Erotica Hotline." *Library Journal*, June 1, 2007, 13.

Jennings, Karlene Noel. "Development is Dysfunctional . . ." *The Bottom Line: Managing Library Finances* 19, no. 4 (2006): 187–88.

Jennings, Karlene Noel, and Jos Wanschers. *Library Development.* SPEC Kit 297. Washington, DC: Association of Research Libraries, 2006.

Kackley, Bob, Pinar Beygo, Jim Miller, and Gloria Chawla. "From Clutter to Cash: Online Book Sales at the University of Maryland's Engineering and Physical Sciences Library (EPSL)." *Collection Management* 31, no. 3 (2006): 73–84.

Kascus, Marie A. "Fundraising for Smaller Academic Libraries: Strategies for Success." *College & Undergraduate Libraries* 10, no. 1 (2003): 1–20.

Kelly, Kathleen S. *Effective Fund-Raising Management.* Mahwah, NJ: Lawrence Erlbaum Associates, 1998.

———. *Fund Raising and Public Relations: A Critical Analysis.* Hillsdale, NJ: Lawrence Erlbaum Associates, 1991.

King, David. "Soliciting Virtual Money." *Library Journal, Net Connect* 125, Issue 14 (Fall 2000): 39–41.

Klein, Kim. *Fundraising for Social Change.* San Francisco: Jossey-Bass, 2007.

Landau, Herbert B. *Winning Library Grants: A Game Plan.* Chicago: American Library Association, 2011.

Lapsley, Andrea R. "Donor Acknowledgement and Recognition: A Not So Simple Thank You." *The Bottom Line: Managing Library Finances* 10, no. 4 (1997): 187–91.

Lehrman, Leonard. "Hear the Music: Concerts in Libraries." *Wilson Library Bulletin* 69, (February 1995): 30–32.

Lopez-Fitzsimmons, Bernadette, and Nicholas Taylor. "Online Newsletters in Academic Libraries." *Catholic Library World* 76, no. 1 (September 2005): 43–48.

Lubrano, John. Comment on the Music Library Association listserv (MLA-L). April 7, 2008. https://listserv.indiana.edu/cgi-bin/wa-iub.exe?A2=MLA-L;MvC6fg;20080407125604-0400A.

MacKellar, Pamela H., and Stephanie K. Gerding. *Winning Grants: A How-to-Do-It Manual for Librarians with Multimedia Tutorials and Grant Development Tools*. New York: Neal-Schuman Publishers, 2010.

Markey, Karen. "Current Educational Trends in the Information and Library Science Curriculum." *Journal of Education for Library and Information Science* 45, no. 4 (Fall 2004): 317–39.

Massey, Tinker. "Management of Gift Materials in an Academic Library." *Collection Building* 24, no. 3 (2005): 80–82.

McKee, John. "What Every Library Can (and Should) Do to Increase Private Support through Planned Gifts." *The Bottom Line: Managing Library Finances* 16, no. 4 (2003): 151–53.

Miller, Michael Page. "Nine and a Half Theses about Fundraising Benefits: Rationalizations, Indulgences, and Opportunity Costs." In *Alternative Revenue Sources: Prospects, Requirements, and Concerns for Nonprofits*, edited by Dwight F. Burlingame and Warren F. Ilchman, 109–17. San Francisco: Jossey-Bass, 1996.

Miller, Robert C. "Endowment Funding in Academic Libraries: Pitfalls and Potential." *The Bottom Line: Managing Library Finances* 1, no. 1 (1987): 23–27.

"Money Matters: Network, Network, Network." *American Libraries* 29, no. 7 (August 1998): 37.

Moore, Christie, and Peter Munstedt. "Brother, Can You Spare a Few Thousand? Raising Money with a Library Newsletter." Poster Session presented at the Music Library Association meeting, Chicago, February 20, 2009. http://musiclibraryassoc2009postersessions.blogspot.com/2009/04/brother-can-you-spare-few-thousand.html.

Munstedt, Peter A. "Library Benefit Concerts: Blood, Sweat, and Cash." *College & Research Libraries News* 50, no. 3 (March 1989): 205–8.

Neal, James G. "College Sports and Library Fundraising." *The Bottom Line: Managing Library Finances* 10, no. 2 (1997): 58–59.

Nichol, Elizabeth. "Out of the Boxes. Treasures from the Donations Pile – Some Hints for Assessment. Notes from an Interactive Session at the IAML(NZ) Conference, Auckland, November 2008, Led by Cathy Williams and Roger Flury of the National Library of New Zealand." *Crescendo: Bulletin of the International Association of Music Libraries* 81 (December 2008): 19–20.

"On eBay, Hoping for a Donor." *Library Journal* 131, no. 5 (March 15, 2006): 13.

Paustenbaugh, Jennifer, and Lynn Trojahn. "Annual Fund Programs for Academic Libraries." *Library Trends* 48, no. 3 (Winter 2000): 579–96.

Quinlan, Catherine. "The Library's Role in the Capital Campaign: Building a Donor Base for the Library." In *Successful Fundraising: Case Studies of Academic Libraries*, edited by Meredith A. Butler, 93–102. Washington, DC: Association of Research Libraries, 2001.

Reed, Sally Gardner, Beth Nawalinski, and Alexander Peterson. *101+ Great Ideas forLibraries and Friends: Marketing, Fundraising, Friends Development, and More!* New York: Neal-Schuman Publishers, 2004.

Ritter, Marian. "The Friends of the Music Library at Western Washington University." *Music Reference Services Quarterly* 9, no. 2 (2005): 55–60.

Rooks, Dana C. "Fund Raising: Random Ramblings. Seek Professional Help." *Journal of Academic Librarianship* 33, no. 2 (March 2007): 292–93.

Rubin, Daniel. "Keeping Count of Charity Mail: Deluged by Solicitations, She Devised an Experiment." *Philadelphia Inquirer*, February 10, 2011, B1, B6.

Ruggiero, Anne, and Julia Zimmerman. "Grateful Recipients: Library Staff as Active Participants in Fund-Raising." *Library Administration & Management* 18, no. 3 (Summer 2004): 140–45.

Schworm, Peter. "Public Libraries Use Internet to Sell Old Books, Help Budgets." *TechNewsWorld*, December 1, 2003, 1–3. http://www.abebooks.com/docs/CompanyInformation/PressRoom/techNewsWorld Dec12003.pdf.

Silverman, Emily. "Beyond Luck and Money: Building Your Base; Identifying Library Donors." *The Bottom Line: Managing Library Finances* 21, no. 4 (2008): 138–41.

Simon, Matthew. "Fundraising as a Small Business Enterprise." *The Bottom Line: Managing Library Finances* 10, no. 2 (1997): 107–11.

Smith, Amy Sherman, and Matthew D. Lehrer. *Legacies for Libraries: A Practical Guide to Planned Giving*. Chicago: American Library Association, 2000.

Steele, Victoria. "The Role of Special Collections in Library Development," In *Library Fundraising: Models for Success*, edited by Dwight F. Burlingame, 72–84. Chicago: American Library Association, 1995.

Steele, Victoria, and Stephen D. Elder. *Becoming a Fundraiser: The Principles and Practice of Library Development*. Chicago: American Library Association, 2000.

Strnad, Benita. "How to Look a Gift Horse in the Mouth, or, How to Tell People You Can't Use Their Old Junk in Your Library." *Collection Building* 14, no. 2 (1995): 29–31.

Swan, James. *Fundraising for Libraries: 25 Proven Ways to Get More Money for Your Library*. New York: Neal-Schuman Publishers, 2002.

Swords, Peter. "How to Read the IRS Form 990." Nonprofit Coordinating Committee of New York website. http://www.npccny.org/new990/new990.htm. Free registration required.

Thompson, Kimberly A., and Karlene Noel Jennings. *More Than a Thank You Note: Academic Library Fundraising for the Dean or Director*. Oxford: Chandos Publishing, 2009.

Vogel, Teri M., and Doug Goans. "Delivering the News with Blogs: The Georgia State University Library Experience." *Internet Reference Services Quarterly* 10, no. 1 (2005): 5–27.

Wachel, Kathy. "Management of Gifts to Libraries. Part IV: Selling Gifts-in-Kind on Consignment; the University of Iowa Libraries Model." *Against the Grain* 14, no. 6 (December 2002/January 2003): 91–92.

Warwick, Mal. *How to Write Successful Fundraising Letters.* San Francisco: Jossey-Bass, 2008.

Watson, Alex. "Library Newsletters in Print and Digital Formats: Faculty Preferences in a Hybrid Format." *Internet Reference Services Quarterly* 16 Issue 4 (2011): 199–210.

Welch, Jeanie M. "The Electronic Welcome Mat: The Academic Library Web Site as a Marketing and Public Relations Tool." *Journal of Academic Librarianship* 31, no. 3 (May 2005): 225–28.

White, Herbert S. "Seeking Outside Funding: The Right and Wrong Reasons." *Library Journal* 117, no. 12 (July 1, 1992): 48–49.

Willis, Paul A., and Paula L. Pope. "Building Endowment through a Major Gifts Program." In *Successful Fundraising: Case Studies of Academic Libraries*, edited by Meredith A. Butler, 61–71. Washington, DC: Association of Research Libraries, 2001.

Winston, Mark D., and Lisa Dunkley. "Leadership Competencies for Academic Librarians: The Importance of Development and Fund-Raising." *College & Research Libraries* 63 (March 2002): 171–82.

Wynbrandt, Robert A. "Musical Performances in Libraries: Is a License from ASCAP Required?" *Public Libraries* 29 (July/August 1990): 224–25.

Zager, Dan. "From the Librarian." *The Sibley Muse: Newsletter of the Sibley Music Library* 27, no. 3 (May 2008): 2–3. http://www.esm.rochester.edu/sibley/muse/SibleyMuse27.3.pdf.

WEB PAGES

All pages were accessed in October 2011 (unless otherwise noted).

American Library Association. "Awards & Grants." http://www.ala.org/ala/awardsgrants/index.cfm.

———. "Code of Ethics of the American Library Association." Adopted in 1939 by the ALA Council; amended June 30, 1981; June 28, 1995; and January 22, 2008. http://www.ala.org/ala/issuesadvocacy/proethics/codeofethics/codeethics.cfm.

———. "Library Fund Raising: A Selected Annotated Bibliography." ALA Library Fact Sheet no. 24. http://www.ala.org/ala/professionalresources/libfactsheets/alalibraryfactsheet24.cfm.

———. "Sending Books to Needy Libraries: Book Donation Programs." ALA Library Fact Sheet no. 12. http://www.ala.org/ala/professionalresources/libfactsheets/alalibraryfactsheet12.cfm.

American Society of Appraisers. http://www.appraisers.org/ASAHome.aspx.

Andrew W. Mellon Foundation. Scholarly Communications and Information Technology. "Overview." http://www.mellon.org/grant_programs/programs/scholarlycommunications#overview.

———. Report from January 1, 2010 through December 31, 2010. http://www.mellon.org/news_publications/annual-reports-essays/annual-reports/content2010.pdf.

Antiquarian Booksellers' Association of America. http://www.abaa.org/books/abaa.

Association for Recorded Sound Collections. Preservation Grants Program (ARSC Grants Committee). "Program for the Preservation of Classical Music Historical Recordings." http://www.arsc-audio.org/preservationgrants.html.

Association of Fundraising Professionals. "Code of Ethical Principals and Standards." http://www.afpnet.org/Ethics/EnforcementDetail.cfm?ItemNumber=3261.

———. "Donor Bill of Rights." http://www.afpnet.org/Ethics/EnforcementDetail.cfm?ItemNumber=3359.

———. "A Survival Kit for Fundraising in Challenging Times." Updated May 25, 2011. http://www.afpnet.org/ResourceCenter/ArticleDetail.cfm?ItemNumber=3942. AFP membership required.

Better World Books. "Our Impact." http://www.betterworldbooks.com/info.aspx?f=our_impact.

Carnegie Library of Pittsburgh. "Friends of the Music Library." accessed April 6, 2012. http://www.clpgh.org/research/music/aboutcollection.html#friends.

Certified Fund Raising Executive. http://www.cfre.org.

Council for Advancement and Support of Education. "CASE Statement of Ethics." http://www.case.org/Samples_Research_and_Tools/Ethics_Resources_and_Issues/CASE_Statement_of_Ethics.html.

Council on Foundations. "Community Foundations." http://www.cof.org/whoweserve/community/index.cfm?navItemNumber=14849.

Department of the Treasury. Internal Revenue Service. "Determining the Value of Donated Property." Publication no. 561. Revised April 2007. http://www.irs.gov/pub/irs-pdf/p561.pdf.

———. Internal Revenue Service. "Charitable Contributions: For Use in Preparing 2010 Returns." Publication no. 526. http://www.irs.gov/pub/irs-pdf/p526.pdf.

———. Internal Revenue Service. "Instructions for Form 8283: Noncash Charitable Contributions." Revised December 2006. http://www.irs.gov/pub/irs-pdf/i8283.pdf.

Facebook. "Causes" (application). http://apps.facebook.com/causes.

Foundation Center. http://foundationcenter.org.

———. "Find Us." http://grantspace.org/Find-Us.

———. *PND: Philanthropy News Digest*. http://foundationcenter.org/pnd.

———. "Requests for Proposals." http://foundationcenter.org/pnd/rfp.

George Mason University. Office of Annual Giving. [General university appeal]. http://www.gmu.edu/development/annual/studentpromo.html.

Gerding, Stephanie, and Pam MacKellar. *Library Grants* (blog). http://librarygrants.blogspot.com.

GrantsAlert.com. http://www.grantsalert.com/about.cfm.

Grants.gov. http://grants.gov.

GuideStar. accessed April 2, 2012. www.guidestar.org.

Harvard University. Loeb Music Library. "History." http://hcl.harvard.edu/libraries/loebmusic/history.html.

Institute of Museum and Library Services. "About Us." http://www.imls.gov/about.

Library Book Sales. http://www.librarybooksales.org.

Massachusetts Institute of Technology. Council for the Arts at MIT (CAMIT). http://arts.mit.edu/about/council.

———. Lewis Music Library. "Class of 1982 Library Fund." http://libraries.mit.edu/music/donations/class1982.html.

———. Lewis Music Library. *What's the Score?* http://libraries.mit.edu/music/news/news-index.html.

———. Sloan Management School. "The MIT Sloan Experience." http://mitsloan.mit.edu/E&I-reunion2007.

Michigan State University. "Grants for Non-Profits: Libraries." http://staff.lib.msu.edu/harris23/grants/2lib.htm.

Music Library Association. "Awards and Grants." http://musiclibraryassoc.org/awards.aspx?id=42.

———. "Donated Music Materials Program." accessed May 24, 2012. http://musiclibraryassoc.org/awards.aspx?id-1001.

Mutter, Anne-Sophie. "Charity Engagement." Anne-Sophie Mutter website. http://www.anne-sophie-mutter.de/benefizkonzerte-karitativ.html?&L=1.

National Endowment for the Humanities. "Recent Grant Awards." http://www.neh.gov/news/recentawards.html.

National Historical Publications and Records Commission. http://www.archives.gov/nhprc.

The Newberry Consort. "About Us." accessed December 30, 2011. http://www.newberryconsort.org/about

Professional Autograph Dealers Association. http://www.padaweb.org.

The Society of American Archivists. "A Guide to Deeds of Gift." accessed April 5, 2012. http://www.archivists.org/publications/deed_of_gift.asp.

Tufts University. "Tisch Talks: The Tisch Library Podcast Series. Episode Four: The Lilly Music Library." April 23, 2007 [date created]. http://www.library.tufts.edu/tisch/tischTalks.html.

University of Florida. "Tour of the Music Library at the University of Florida." May 5, 2008 [date created]. http://www.youtube.com/watch?v=RhzgYIRjwr4.

University of South Carolina. USC Music Library Blog. Episode 1: Hit Us Up. September 20, 2007 [date created]. accessed April 28, 2012. http://youtube.com/watch?v=YHPeZS4g-QU.

University of Waterloo. "Library Campaign." http://www.lib.uwaterloo.ca/develop/kresge_flash.

Western Washington University Music Library. Friends of the Music Library. *High Notes*. http://library.wwu.edu/page/4540

INDEX

A
ABEbooks.com, 48
Academic Library Advancement and Development Network, 4
Adamstown Area (PA) Library Friends, 52
advisory councils to libraries, 12
AFP. *See* Association of Fundraising Professionals
ALA. *See* American Library Association
ALADN. *See* Academic Library Advancement and Development Network
alumni, approaching through music department, 6, 83; association, 25; generosity of, 19, 79, 81–83; identifying, 11; loyalty of, 16, 74, 83, 86; mailing list, 12, 13, 80; nondonors, 24–25, 107; ownership of, 11; performing in concert, 44; promoting library to, 7–8; telephoning, 24
Amazon.com, 48
American Library Association, 5, 50, 66, 74, 111
American Society of Appraisers, 109
American University, University Library, "Music Library: Gifts and Donations," 89
annual funds, 24–25
annuities, 38
antiquarian book market, 50
Antiquarian Booksellers' Association of America, 109
appraisals, 35, 109
apps for raising money, 20
ARL. *See* Association of Research Libraries
ARSC. *See* Association for Recorded Sound Collections
ARTstor, 58
"the ask," 25–26
Association for Healthcare Philanthropy, 74
Association for Recorded Sound Collections, 5, 67
Association of Fundraising Professionals, 4, 74, 105
Association of Research Libraries, 1
athletics and fundraising, 25, 110
auctions, online, 49, 111–112

B
benefit concerts. *See* concerts
Bennent, Anne, 24
bequests, 37

Better World Books, 49
Billings, Mary, 49
blogs, 7, 16, 17, 80
book endowments. *See* collection endowments
book sales, 47–51; appeal of music materials, 49–50; legal restrictions, 50–51; testing the value of, 47–48
bookplates, 30–31; electronic, 31, 86
booksellers, online, 48–49
Browar, Lisa, 37
Brothers, Melanie, 79

C
capacity rating (donors), 15
capital campaigns, 25, 108
Carnegie Classification of Institutions of Higher Education, 17
Carnegie Library of Pittsburgh, Friends of the Music Library, 52
CASE. *See* Council for Advancement and Support of Education
case statements, 21, 26
Catholic University of America, University Libraries, "Gift Policy for the Music Library," 90–91
Causes (Facebook app), 20
Certified Fund Raising Executive, 4
CFRE. *See* Certified Fund Raising Executive
challenge grant, 61
charitable gift annuity, 38
charitable giving in U.S., 11
charitable lead trust, 38
charitable remainder annuity trust, 38
charitable remainder trust, 38
charitable remainder unitrust, 38
charities, aggressive fundraising tactics, 108; libraries donating materials to, 50
Chinese Club, 13
class reunions, 83
Code of Ethics (American Library Association), 74
collection endowments, 40, 85–86
community and local organizations providing grants, 67

125

concerts, benefit, 43–46, 110–111; free, 47, 87; Library of Congress, 43; organizing, 44–46
consignment book sales, 48
constituency of libraries, 11
contact reports, 15
contracts (gifts), 34–35, 101
Corporate Giving Online, 57
corporations (grants), 56–57
Corson-Finnerty, Adam, 23
Cosby, Bill, 110
cost-benefit analysis, 34
Council for Advancement and Support of Education, 4, 74
Council for the Arts at MIT, 66, 86–87
Cow Pie Bingo, 51–52
Craig, Lois, 86
CRAT. *See* charitable remainder annuity trust
CRUT. *See* charitable remainder unitrust
cultivation, of donors, 15–21; of library administration and development staff, 22
cycle of service, promotion, and fundraising, 8–9

D

data mining, 15
deed of gift. *See* contracts (gifts)
deferred charitable gift annuity, 38
deferred giving. *See* planned giving
development staff, 3–7; asking for donations, 21, 25–26, 71, 83; conflicting goals with library staff, 73, 75; cooperation of music department, 6, 83; disparities with librarians, 4; librarians' cultivation of, 22; methods of analyzing donors, 15; overseeing events, 52–53; performing specialized work, 13, 34, 36, 37, 71; prompt communication, 30; qualifications and traits, 3–5; synergy with librarians, 5; turnover, 5; understanding librarians' mistakes, 73; working with proposals, 8, 14, 21
Directory of Music Foundations, 2009–2010, 60–61
Division of Preservation and Access (NEH), 63
Division of Public Programs (NEH), 63
Division of Research Programs (NEH), 63
donation forms (online), 23
donations, 33–41
Donor Bill of Rights, 74
donors, abusing privileges, 74–75; capacity rating, 15; competition for, 6, 16; cultivating, 15–21; expectations, 26–27; finding gift opportunities, 8; "helicopter," 40–41; identifying, 11–15; influence in library, 40–41, 75; major, 14–15, 20–21, 28, 29, 31, 52–53, 107; motivations to give, 37; offered enticements, 114; public acknowledgment of, 51, 81; relationship with librarians, 15–16; small, 22–23; soliciting, 12, 22–27; stewarding, 27–32; taking donations back, 41, 110; viewpoints opposed to librarians, 75–76

E

East Carolina University, Joyner Library, "Donations to the Music Library," 92
eBay, 49, 112
economic environment, 15
Eda Kuhn Loeb Music Library (Harvard University), 41
electronic bookplates. *See* bookplates
"Encore Concerts" (benefit), 44
endowed funds, 36
endowed music library chair, 41
endowments, 39–41, 85–86
e-mail, means of communication, 19, 31, 80
Epstein, David, 83
ethics, concerns, 73–76; codes of, 73–74
events, 43–53; for major donors, 52–53
expendable funds, 36

F

Facebook, music libraries' use of, 106; promoting library with, 7, 19; sending library news with, 80; use in fundraising, 20, 31
faculty members, adding to mailing list, 12; assistance in fundraising, 6; contacting for grant money, 13; performing at library events, 44, 47, 51; preference for newsletters, 105; telephoning retired, 24; thanking donors, 28, 30, 85
fees on monetary gifts, 36
Fenner, Audrey, 47–48
financial reasons for fundraising, 2
Fischer, Marilyn, 74
flash presentations, 19
Fontaine, Sue, 8
Foundation Center resources, 57, 60
Foundation Center Cooperating Collections, 60
Foundation Directory (print and online), 60
foundations (grants), 57–61; community, 58; company-sponsored, 58; family, 58; independent, 58; operating, 58; pursuing a grant, 59–61
free concerts. *See* concerts

French, Richard F., 41
friends of the library, adding to mailing list, 12; annual fund drives, 25; assistance of, 13; events, 52; issuing newsletter, 18; selling books, 48–49; value of, 52
Frisby, Anthony J., 17
fundraising, detrimental to library, 72–73; hidden costs, 69–71; hierarchical administrative structure, 3, 26; improves library standing, 72; initiation of, 2; long-term process, 22–23; librarian mistakes, 73; number of music librarians participating in, 1; priorities, 14; proposals, 8; reason for, 73; resources on campus, 13–14; too much success, 72; use of term versus "development," 103
funds, restricted and unrestricted, 36

G
Gerding, Stephanie, 48, 61
gifts in kind, 33–36, 86–87; contracts and policies, 34–35; hidden cost of, 34, 70; selection process, 34, 76; solicited, 33; tax deductions, 35; unsolicited, 33–34
giving links (online), 23
Giving Institute, 74
Gornish, Stanley E., 16
government grants, 56, 62–66; administration of, 65–66; application process, 64–65; receiving application advice from agencies, 65
grant payment options, 61
grants, 55–67; institutional approval to write, 55–56; local opportunities, 66–67
Grants for Arts, Culture, & the Humanities, 2011 Digital Edition, 60
Grants for Libraries & Information Services, 2011 Digital Edition, 60
Grants for Libraries Hotline, 61
GrantsAlert.com, 61
GuideStar, 58

H
Half.com, 48
Harbison, John, 79
Harris, Ellen T., 79–80
Heath, Kristin, 35
helicopter donors. *See* donors
Herther, Nancy K., 61
hidden costs. *See* fundraising

High Notes (Western Washington University Music Library newsletter), 18
Huang, Samuel T., 3

I
IAML. *See* International Association of Music Libraries, Archives and Documentation Centres
IAML-US Donated Music Materials Program, 50
identification of donors, 11–15
IMLS. *See* Institute of Museum and Library Services
information-resource endowments, 40
installment payments, 36
Institute of Museum and Library Services, 62, 63
institutional approval of grants, 55–56
institutional politics, 71–73
Internal Revenue Service, 35–36, 45, 50–51, 57–58; Form 8283, 35; Form 8282, 35; Form 990PF, 58; Section 501(c)(3), 57
International Association of Music Libraries, Archives and Documentation Centres, 5, 50
iPads, 82
IRS. *See* Internal Revenue Service

J
Jennings, Karlene Noel, 52
JSTOR, 58

K
Kelly, Kathleen S., 75, 103
Kipnis, Daniel G., 17
Klein, Kim, 17

L
Lancaster (PA) Area Library, 48
Larson, Forrest, 84–85
lectures (events), 51
Lehrman, Leonard, 43
legal restrictions for book sales, 50–51
letter campaign, 52
letters of support for grants, 65
Lewis Music Library. *See* Massachusetts Institute of Technology
Lewis, Rosalind Denny, 80
library administration, librarians' cultivation of, 22
Library Book Sales (website), 49
library budget, monitoring decreased funding, 76
library director, 3, 25, 28
"Library Erotica Hotline," 24

Library Grants blog, 61
library mission statement, 3, 43, 77
Library of Congress concert series, 43
Library Services and Technology Act (LSTA), 62
library science curriculum offering fundraising, 103
library staff, added responsibilities, 69–70; jealousy, 71; profiting from fundraising, 76; questioning value of fundraising, 73; relationship with users, 70–71; role in promoting library, 7
library users, equal treatment of, 74–75
license fees for music performances, 45, 46, 111
life insurance, 38
life-income gifts, 38
links, online donations, 23, 107
local organizations (grants). *See* community and local organizations providing grants
LSTA. *See* Library Services and Technology Act
Lubrano, John, 109

M

MacKellar, Pamela H., 61
mailing list, 12–13
major donors. *See* donors
marketing, 1, 8–9, 103, 104
Massachusetts Institute of Technology, Banjo Club, 82; Charles Hayden Memorial Library, 79; Class of 1982, 19, 81–83; Museum, 82; Provost Office, 6; Rosalind Denny Lewis Music Library, 18, 19, 47, 66, 79–87; School of Humanities and Social Science, 6; Symphony Orchestra (MITSO), 6, 83–84
matching gifts, 36, 57
matching grants, 61
Mellon Foundation, 58–59
Merkey, Terra, 35
Mikita, Elizabeth G., 17
misers, elderly library-loving, 15
Missouri State University Libraries, 24
Missouri Western State College, St. Joseph, 48
MIT. *See* Massachusetts Institute of Technology
MITSO. *See* Massachusetts Institute of Technology Symphony Orchestra
MLA. *See* Music Library Association
MLA-L (Music Library Association's e-mail distribution list), 50, 103
MLA Survey of Personnel Characteristics, 2009 Report and Statistical Summary, 1
monetary gifts, 36, 75

moral dilemmas, 74–76
MSA. *See* Museum Services Act
Museum Services Act, 62
Music at MIT Oral History Project, 84–85
music department development staff, 5–7, 13, 83
"Music in Stacks," 47
music libraries, role on campus, 11–12
Music Library Association, 1, 5, 66, 74
Mutter, Anne-Sophie, 44, 110–11
MySpace, 19

N

naming, opportunities, 39; rights to a library, 49, 112
NARA. *See* National Archives and Records Administration
National Archives and Records Administration, 62
National Directory of Corporate Giving, 57
National Leadership Grants (IMLS), 62
Nassau (NY) Library System, 43
National Committee on Planned Gifts, 37
National Endowment for the Humanities, 62–63
National Historical Publications and Records Commission, 62–63
NEH. *See* National Endowment for the Humanities
Neil Ratliff IAML Outreach Grant, 50
network media, 19–20
Newberry Consort (Newberry Library), 44, 110
newsletters, 7, 17–19, 28, 52, 80–81, 105
NHPRC. *See* National Historical Publications and Records Commission

O

Office of Digital Humanities (NEH), 63
Ohio State University, University Libraries, Music and Dance, "Support the Library," 93
one-time donations, 39
online auctions. *See* auctions, online
online booksellers. *See* booksellers, online
oral history. *See* Music at MIT Oral History Project
outside users, 12, 74–75
overhead for grants, 56

P

passive approach to solicitation. *See* solicitation of donors
personal contact, 20, 83
Philanthropy News Digest, 61
planned giving, 36–38

photography at concerts, 46
podcasts, 19, 106
politics, institutional, 2–3
pooled endowments, 41
pooled income fund, 38
principal investigator (grants), 65
Professional Autograph Dealers Association, 109
professional societies and associations providing grants, 66–67
project narrative (grants), 65
projects, one-time donations supporting, 39
Prokopoff, Stephen, 86
promoting the library, 7–9
proposals, 8, 14, 21
prospect manager, 3, 25–26
prospects, 11, 13, 15, 21
public relations, 8–9
publicity for concerts, 46

Q

Queens College Music Library [City University of New York], Aaron Copland School of Music, "Giving: Support the Library," 94–95

R

rating system (donors), 15
receptions for concerts, 46
recording concerts, 46
rejecting donations, 27, 34–35, 40, 75
renovations of music library (MIT), 6, 79–80, 81–82
restricted endowments, 40
restricted funds, 36
"Restore a Score" program (Royal College of Music), 23, 97
RFPs (requests for proposals), 61
Ritter, Marian, 18, 52
Robison, Brian, 47
Rolling Stones, 77
Royal College of Music Library, 23, 96–97
Ruggiero, Anne, 71

S

Scholarly Communications and Information Technology Program (Mellon Foundation), 59
Seattle Symphony, 52
"second ask" campaign, 25
seed grants, 61
selling music library materials, 49–50

service, library, 8–9
Sibley Muse (Eastman School of Music newsletter), 18
Simon, Matthew, 23
social media, 19–20
solicitation of donors, 12, 22–27; passive approach, 22–23
sound recording reformatting project, 83–84
sports. *See* athletics and libraries
staff positions, supported by endowments, 41
start-up money (grants), 61
Steele, Victoria, 5
stewardship of donors, 27–32, 81–83
Streit, Samuel A., 37
student assistants, 13
student government association, 13–14

T

tax, advice, 26; deductions, 14, 35–36, 45, 50–51; tax-exempt status of libraries, 51
technology, influence on donations, 20
telephone calls, 31; solicitation, 23–24
thanks, ongoing expressions of, 31
thank-you letters, 27–30, 46
theft of library materials, 49
Thompson, Kimberly A., 52
tours, library, 30, 106
trusts, 38
Tsou, Judy, 24
Tucson-Pima (AZ) Public Library friends group, 48
Twitter, 7, 20

U

UCLA Library, Music Library, "Giving to the Music Library," 98
University of Hawaii at Manoa, 111
University of Iowa, 48
University of Maryland, Baltimore County, Media Department, 13–14
University of Maryland, Engineering and Physical Sciences Library, 48
University of Mississippi, 105
University of Missouri-Kansas City Conservatory Library, 44
University of North Carolina at Greensboro, 47–48
University of South Carolina, University Libraries, Music Library, "Gift Policy," 99
University of Washington Music Library, 24
university resources for grants, 66

unrestricted endowments, 40
unrestricted funds, 36, 81
used book dealers, 50

V

Vancouver Opera, 52
Veni Creator Spiritus, 79
videos, promotional, 19
volunteers, assistance with renovation, 79; book sales, 48; events, 52; from corporations, 56–57; students, 24, 79

W

Washington University Libraries, Gaylord Music Library, "Donations," 100; "Special Collections: Sample Deed of Gift," 101
"Waves of Pleasure," 47
websites, cultivation through, 16; donor policies on, 35, 74; for book sales, 49; grant information on, 66; used for fundraising, 20, 23
Western Oregon University, 111
Western Washington University Friends of the Music Library, 18, 52
What's the Score? (MIT Lewis Music Library newsletter), 18, 80–81
Willis, Paul A., 19
wills. *See* bequests
widgets, 20
wugging, 20

Y

YouTube, 19, 106

Z

Zimmerman, Julia, 71